THEOLOGIANS AND AUTHORITY

WITHIN THE LIVING CHURCH

James J. Mulligan

THE POPE JOHN CENTER

186 FORBES ROAD
BRAINTREE, MASSACHUSETTS

Imprimatur:
The Most Rev. Thomas J. Welsh, D.D.
Bishop of Allentown
28 July 1986

Library of Congress Cataloging-in-Publication Data

Mulligan, James J.
    Theologians and authority within the living church.

    Bibliography: p.
    Includes indexes.
        1. Catholic Church—Teaching office.   2. Church.
3. Theologians.   4. Catholic Church—Doctrines.
I. Title.
BX1746.M85   1986   262'.8   86-30542
ISBN 0-935372-18-0 (pbk.)

Contents

ACKNOWLEDGEMENTS

Curran, Charles E., "Anxiety in the Academy," *The Tablet,* 9 November 1985, p. 1177, London, England.

Curran, Charles E., *Ongoing Revision,* © 1976 by Fides/Claretian Press, Chicago, Illinois.

Curran, Charles E., *Transition and Tradition in Moral Theology,* © 1979 by University of Notre Dame Press.

Ford, John C., SJ, and Kelly, Gerald, SJ, "Doctrinal Value and Interpretation of Papal Teaching," *Readings in Moral Theology No. 3,* Paulist Press (originally in *Contemporary Moral Theology I,* Newman Press, 1958).

Flannery, Austin, OP, *Vatican Council II: Conciliar and Post-Conciliar Documents,* St. Paul Editions, Boston, 1976; © Costello Publishing Company, Inc., Northport, New York, 1975.

Grisez, Germain, *The Way of The Lord Jesus,* Volume I, Franciscan Herald Press, Chicago, Illinois 1983.

Johnston, William, SJ, *The Cloud of Unknowing,* Doubleday and Company, Image Books, 1973.

Jurgens, W.A., *The Faith of the Early Fathers,* The Liturgical Press, Collegeville, Minnesota, 1970.

Lewis, C.S., *Mere Christianity,* Macmillan, New York, New York, 1943, 1966, © Collins Publishers, London, England.

Lewis, C.S., *The Problem of Pain,* Macmillan, New York, New York, 1940, 1962, ©
Collins Publishers, London, England.

Lewis, C.S., "Transposition," in *The Weight of Glory,* Wm. B. Eerdmans Publishing
Company, Grand Rapids, Michigan, 1966, © Collins Publishers, London,
England

MacDonald, George, reprinted from *Creation in Christ,* Rolland Hein ed., by permission of Harold Shaw Publishers. Copyright © 1976 by Harold Shaw
Publishers.

Musurillo, Herbert A., SJ, *The Fathers of the Primitive Church,* Mentor-Omega Edition, © New American Library, New York, New York, 1966.

Quasten, Johannes, *Patrology,* 3 volumes, Christian Classics, Westminster, Maryland, 1960–1962.

Robinson, John A.T., reprinted from *The Body: A Study in Pauline Theology.* © SCM
Press Ltd. 1952. Reprinted and used by permission of the Wesminster Press,
Philadelphia, Pennsylvania. International rights granted by SCM Press Ltd.,
London, England.

Ratzinger, Joseph Cardinal, "The Church and the Theologians," reprinted in *Origins: NC Documentary Service,* 8 May 1986, Volume 15, No. 47. © University
of Saint Michael's College, Toronto, Ontario, Canada.

Biblical quotations, unless otherwise noted, are taken from: J.M. Powis Smith and
Edgar J. Goodspeed, *The Complete Bible: An American Translation,* The University of Chicago Press, Chicago, Illinois, 1923, 1927, 1948. Sixteenth impression 1960.

FOREWORD

Proper interpretation of the Sacred Scriptures demands that we try to ascertain the historical circumstances in which a book was written, the kind of literature with which we are dealing and, insofar as possible, the intent of the inspired author. One of the few places in Scripture where the author himself clearly tells us what he intends is in the Second Book of Maccabees. This author writes to proclaim god's wonders, wrought on behalf of his people during the last days of their domination by the Seleucid successors of Alexander the Great, less than two centuries before the birth of Jesus. He writes:

> Now the story of Judas Maccabeus and his brothers, and the purification of the great temple, and the rededication of the altar, and also of the wars with Antiochus Epiphanes and his son Eupator, and the heavenly manifestations shown to those who zealously championed the Jewish religion, so that few as they were, they plundered the whole country and drove out the barbarian hordes and recovered the world renowned temple, and freed the city, and restored the laws which were on the point of being destroyed, since the Lord, with great forbearance had shown mercy to them—all this, as related by Jason of Cyrene in five books, we will try to condense into one volume. For in view of the flood of statistics and

the difficulty created by the abundance of the material, for those who wish to plunge into the historical narratives, we have aimed at attracting those who like to read, and at making it easy for those who are disposed to memorize, and at being of use to all our readers. For us, who have taken upon ourselves the painful task of abridgment, the thing is not easy, and takes sweat and midnight oil, just as it is no easy matter for a man who prepares a banquet and strives to benefit others. Still, to win the gratitude of so many, we will gladly endure the painful task, leaving to the historian the investigation of details, but taking pains to follow the lines of an epitome. (II Mac 2, 19–28)

It seemed to me that if an inspired author could take the time to introduce his purposes, so, too, could I. The historical circumstances of the writing are easy enough to grasp, since we live in the midst of them. It is, as Dickens said, the best of times; it is the worst of times. All of which, I suppose, depends upon your point of view or those with whom you talk. In reality, I think it is neither, but is probably just a normal time, like all the times that have preceded us and which are yet to come. It is a time of learned discussion and a time of heated dispute. It is a time of renewal and a time of conflict. But this has been the case throughout the history of Christianity. The forms of renewal differ (else, how could they be renewal?) but the fact is always there. The contents of the disputes differ, but there is always some tension in life. In our own times much of the dispute seems to center (within the Catholic Church) on the relationship between authority and theology—between Magisterium and theologians. It is within this historical circumstance that I would like to address myself.

As to the kind of literature with which you are now dealing, it is an attempt to present in clear and readable language the problems attendant upon the historical circumstances and what I see in terms of solution. It is not intended to be a highly technical book, even though I have tried to make use of solid sources upon which to build. More academic elements are generally relegated to the footnotes, and there I have tried to supply at least some suggestions of further literature which will interest those who wish to plunge into the deeper waters. The text makes use of that information but is written—I hope—so as to sustain the interest even of the reader not zealously inclined to technicalities.

The intent of the author (who in this case can lay no claim to divine inspiration)? My intention is to answer some questions that have been raised about the proper place of authority and theology in the Catholic Church. Such questions—and the necessary answers—demand that we begin to examine them in a particular context with a specific point of view. The way in which we look at things can make all the difference in the world when it comes to our assessment of them. I have attempted in the course of the book to describe such a point of view and to present it in a way that I hope will appeal to the experience of Christian life, an experience which we all share. In my presentation I will, of course, have to deal with opinions and conclusions which may be the opposite of my own. Even though this is the case, my intent is not primarily polemical, even though I find it necessary to adduce arguments for what I say. Instead, my main intent is to explain, to clarify and to share with the reader a context within which I think there can be peace. My intention is not to win an argument, but to set out a fair presentation of matters which I see as true and essential.

There is far more to be said about the subjects raised in the book than can be contained within it. There were some chapters which could easily have been developed into books of their own. But one can do only so much. There is need for abbreviation. So let us begin the book itself. As the Author of Second Maccabees also said:

> Here then let us begin the story, without adding more to what has already been said; for it is foolish to write a long preface to the history and then abbreviate the history itself. (II Mac 2, 32)

James J. Mulligan
Mount Saint Mary's Seminary
Emmitsburg, Maryland

Chapter 1

A Point of View

When I was a boy growing up in Northeastern Pennsylvania, our father would often take the whole family for a ride on a Sunday afternoon. A few of these excursions were to Delaware Water Gap—a gorge cut through the foothills of the Appalachians by the gentle erosion of the Delaware River. There was, as I recall, a point in the drive at which one could see not only the gorge itself, but, near the top, a rock outcropping in the shape of a profile of a man's face. I can remember how we used to watch for and each time be impressed by that craggy countenance. It could be seen only from one particular vantage point. From any other angle, all we saw was the cliff—impressive enough, but without that special face. The point of view was essential.

J.R.R. Tolkien, in his essay, "On Fairy-Stories," deals with the fairy tale as literary form.[1] He speaks of elements of the fairy tale, which he defines as Recovery, Escape and Consolation. The tale sets forth a reality within the setting of an unfamiliar and magical world. To that world we are allowed to escape as we enter the story, and in those familiar surroundings we come to grips with values that, in our own everyday world, we see with the eyes of easy familiarity. A new point of view sets into sharp relief what we so easily take for granted as we view life from

1

the comfortable perspective of our daily routine. In this new context we are offered the gift of Recovery. We see that which has become for us mundane in a frame of reference that makes us examine it anew and wonder at its worth. From this comes the Consolation, the happy ending, the return to our own world with an old-new value in our possession.

Tolkien tells us that this newness of perspective comes not only through literature, but also through the humility of one who is willing to examine his world with new eyes. He speaks of this ability as *Mooreeffoc* or the Chestertonian Fantasy. Chesterton had spoken of it as the capacity to grasp the strangeness of familiar things once they are seen from a new aspect. The word, Mooreeffoc, he drew from Dickens who had seen and been surprised by this foreign sounding word which appeared in every town and city in his time—and indeed is not an unfamiliar word even in our own. Yet one can see it only from that vantage point of being inside a Coffeeroom and looking out through the window upon which the word is painted. The familiar is suddenly new, unfamiliar, a challenge to the imagination. The dull, old gem in the family heirloom, when seen in a new setting, takes on a new lustre.

One's vantage point is meaningful, then, in viewing the world around us, in the realm of literature, and even in its capacity to open our eyes to the unexpectedness of the expected. Yet the importance of the point of view may, in fact, be of much deeper significance than even these examples would lead us to think. On a number of occasions C.S. Lewis was invited to preach and it was in one such instance that he delivered a Pentecost sermon in Mansfield College Chapel, Oxford. This was later published under the title, "Transposition."[2] Here the concept of a "point of view" leads to a new depth of understanding of the relation between the natural and the supernatural.

Although I shall not, for the most part, be quoting directly from Lewis' presentation, I wish clearly to acknowledge him as the source of the line of thought I shall now attempt to develop. I, too, will begin with a passage that he quotes and from which he leads the reader to new and deeper insights. It is taken from *Pepys's Diary:*

> With my wife to the Kings's House to see *The Virgin Martyr*, and it is mighty pleasant . . . But that which did please me beyond anything in the whole world was the wind musick when the angel comes down, which is so sweet that it ravished me and indeed, in a word, did wrap up my soul so that it made me really sick, just as I have formerly been when in love with my wife . . . and makes me resolve to practise wind musick and make my wife do the like. (Feb. 27, 1668.)

This is, one must admit, an odd statement. What was he talking about? How are we to interpret the fact that the beauty of the music made him "really sick"? That he had felt the same "when in love with [his] wife"? And even that he wanted to feel this same sickness in the future? What Lewis suggests is that he is attempting to describe an internal sensation with which we are all familiar.

Have you ever felt a sort of flutter in your stomach? It comes and goes at various times. Have you ever sat in the waiting room of a dentist, hoping that your turn would come soon and that, at the same time, it would not come at all? That nervous little flutter in the stomach is usually even more pronounced once the receptionist points at you and says, "The Doctor will see *you* now." Or have you ever waited at a terminal for an old friend to arrive—someone for whom you care a great deal and have missed for a long time? Again, that little flutter, amplified as you finally move forward to welcome the smiling friend who advances from the plane. Finally, there is that old familiar flutter in another, and thoroughly different, situation. I can remember it well from one occasion many years ago. I had arrived as a young student in Naples, on my way to Rome. Those who had come to welcome us had also arranged that we would have a day on Capri. The return trip from Capri was made in a wind that raised the waves in the Bay of Naples and there was a whole epidemic of stomach flutters among us who were aboard. It was a flutter of the kind that brought out not only an internal sensation but a brigade of sailors with mops and buckets as well, since there were simply too many people to be easily accommodated at the rail.

What shall we conclude? Since in every instance there was that same old flutter, shall we say that an hour with the dentist is a delight? That seasickness fills us with happiness? Or that we are nauseated by old friends? Our bodies and our emotions are, together, expressing a variety of internal states and we are not likely at all to mistake one for the other, even though that flutter accompanied all of them.

There is a similarity with what happens when one translates texts from one language to another. For example, the range of vocabulary necessary to write a book on nuclear physics is far wider than that which had been needed to produce the Hebrew Old Testament. The Hebrew text got along admirably with a vocabulary of about 800 basic roots. The nuclear physicist could hardly be expected to produce an intelligible work within the same limitations. But suppose that he were asked to do so? That he were asked to translate his work into Biblical Hebrew. Would it be possible? I suppose that it would, provided that the translator were given some latitude in his use of words. Words might have to do double duty and serve with one meaning in one context and another meaning in another. Provided that this were explained clearly to the reader, it might be possible to accomplish the goal of translation. The final result might fall short of the original in its clarity and versatility, but it could still be adequate to the occasion, at least within its own built-in limits.

Lewis makes use of this sort of linguistic example, and he then goes on to say:

> I take our emotional life to be "higher" than the life of our
> sensations—not, of course, morally higher, but richer, more varied,

more subtle. And this is a higher level which nearly all of us know. And I believe that if anyone watches carefully the relation between his emotions and his sensations he will discover the following facts: (1) that the nerves do respond, and in a sense most adequately and exquisitely, to the emotions; (2) that their resources are far more limited, the possible variations of sense far fewer, than those of emotion; (3) and that the senses compensate for this by using the *same* sensation to express more than one emotion—even, as we have seen, to express opposite emotions.[3]

If one were to see only the flutter and nothing more than that, then there would be no difference at all in the internal events described above. But to one who observes the realities from within, there is a distinct difference and the more subtle varieties of emotion give widely differing meanings to the same old flutter. In other words, the lower (or less subtle) level can only be understood and interpreted in light of the higher.

Lewis speaks of another example that is easy to grasp. Painting and drawing is an effort to capture the three dimensional within two dimensions. The same sorts of triangular shapes may represent a clown's hat, a gabled roof or a perspective view of a road going off into the distance. *Trompe l'oeil* attempts to represent three dimensions within two so realistically that the viewer is fooled into thinking that he is seeing the real object. I have seen paintings in some houses in Europe that so vividly represent the image of a door with a stairway or corridor going into the distance that you discover the illusion only when you attempt to use the door. If we were inhabitants of no more than two dimensions, then triangular shapes would be no more to us than triangles and there would be no illusion in the painted doorway. Yet, because we know the reality of a three dimensional world, we interpret the art and can grasp its representative significance. Our experience of a higher level makes it possible to capture it, to some extent, in the lower, and the inadequacies of the lower are in some way overcome.

There is in these instances a "transposition." The shades of meaning in emotion are transposed into a lower, physical level which lacks the same potentiality for variations. Yet it is the emotion itself which is expressed in the physical response. In the one case the flutter *is* joy and in another case it *is* nausea. The same can be said of the painting. It not only represents the three dimensional object, but it is itself a part of that same three dimensional world. Because we, too, are part of that world, we are capable of grasping the intended representation even in its two dimensional presentation.

Transposition, however, can give us a still deeper insight and can be seen at work in an area that turns out to be far more theological. We are creatures who contain within ourselves a number of levels—levels which we share with other, lesser creatures. As living beings we need nourishment, and this is a reality that we share with lower forms of life. All living things, in one way or another, ingest nutrients. Recall the days of your high school biology classes. You looked through a microscope at an amoeba. Its movement, without the same elegance perhaps, was not totally unlike the locomotion of Henry Higgins' rival philologist. Oozing charm from every pore, it oiled its way around the floor. And as the amoeba, constantly changing its shape, slides around its microcosm, bits of nutrition are surrounded and absorbed into its single cell. It ingests nutrients.

Higher forms of life, such as plants, also ingest nutrients. The mode is quite different from that of the Amoeba. Nutrition is taken in through roots and carried through the plant in a very complex venous system. Nourishment, water and light are all combined in a process of photosynthesis and the raw ingredients of nutrition are transformed into the living plant itself. Trees don't slide around the ground and surround their food in the manner of the amoeba. On the other hand, they do, in common with protozoan life, ingest nutrients.

Have you ever raised house plants? If so, you may have used plant food of different kinds. You put it into the pot and the plant absorbs it through its roots. But have you ever seen the plant smack its roots over a particularly tasty bit of nourishment? or wag its leaves when it saw you coming with its fertilizer? Have you ever kept a cat or a dog? They too ingest nutrients. But you know, from experience, that the cat or dog does express its appreciation of its food and will accept some and reject others. The finicky cat of the television commercials is not just a product of Madison Avenue's imagination. The advertising is merely cashing in on a fact. Animals not only ingest nutrients, but the higher animals express preferences. While the plant will sop up whatever is thrown into the pot, the dog or cat may examine what you have put into its dish, give you an accusatory and disappointed glare, and stalk off until you come to your senses. The ingestion of nutrients has been further refined by the addition of a sense of taste. It is still the same old ingestion, in common with the amoeba, but it is also something new.

Human beings are animals. Human beings ingest nutrients. Human beings have taste, and so have likes and dislikes. But the human being brings to the ingestion of nutrients a dimension that the plants and animals cannot even conjecture. Apart from the tinny tones of the science fiction robot, can you imagine a young man calling his fiancee and saying, "Would you like to go out on Saturday evening and ingest nutrients?" The implications of an invitation to dinner are certainly not limited to the nutritional. The couple may go to a restaurant and ingest nutrients, but there is now present a dimension of meaning that far surpasses any of the levels we have looked at. The quality of the *personal* adds a dimension which takes a lower reality and imbues it with a new and higher life. There is a reality which is symbolic, an expression of care, of concern, of love. In fact, once we leave the technical language of the scientist (and apart from ways in which one might choose to speak of the comatose) human eating sounds silly when described merely as ingestion of nutrients. Indeed, in the sharing of a meal there is something more than even the symbolic. One might refer to it, in a way, as sacramental. The act of eating together makes present a reality which far surpasses the eating in itself.

This sacramental reality, of course, finds its highest expression in the Eucharist. Here again there is the act of ingesting nutrients. It is the same old, familiar act that we have been looking at all along. Yet the dimension of meaning has been drawn into a totally new realm. Now our meal is nourishment, it is sign or symbol, but it is still more. It is now the sacramental sign which produces what it signifies and it unites us with the risen Jesus. But notice that even at this level it has not ceased to contain within itself all the preceding levels. It is still all that it was and even more. This is what we mean by transposition.

Look now at our way of viewing this reality. When we see the Eucharist from the viewpoint of biological life, then it is nothing more than the ingestion of nutrients. When we see it from the human level of the meal, it is sign or symbol. But when seen from the vantage point of faith, it is the presence of Christ himself. In other words, the reality of transposition can only be appreciated when viewed from the highest level. The point of view is essential.

We can gain still further insight if we reflect on the fact that our knowledge itself has various levels. Again we see the value of the point of view. Everyone is familiar with the fable of the blind men describing the elephant. Each touched a different part of it. The one who touched its trunk was convinced that the elephant was much like a snake. The one who touched its leg was certain that it was not unlike a tree trunk. The one who touched its ear found it a broad and leafy sort of being. Each knew a part, and "saw" the whole only from that point of view.

Suppose we were to ask the cytologist for a description of a human being? He could be quite accurate indeed, but his description would center on the working and interworking of cellular structures, and man is far more than that. The biologist could describe him as one among a variety of life forms, but if his description were limited to the physically biological and to that alone, then we would know little about his mind. If the psychologist were giving the description, we would begin at last to learn about his mind, his emotions, his power to love. But even this would not be all, since we would not have learned of his spirit and its capacity to know and love in union with God. The one who truly knows his heart and soul is the one who would have to give the final, and best, description, and this could come only from the viewpoint of faith. Each ascending description would have to take into account the preceding ones, but only the last could produce the most complete description.

There is here, too, a transposition. The lower knowledge is taken up into and given new dimensions of meaning by the higher. When we come to any effort to see the real meaning of mankind, each of the sciences can make its contribution, but none by itself can give the fully satisfying explanation. In fact, even theology, were we to see it as the highest of the sciences in this regard, cannot give us the final answer. There is still greater transposition.

In the Fourteenth Century a mystic, whose name is unknown to us, wrote a book called *The Cloud of Unknowing*. He is concerned with prayer, with contemplation of God. Only in this contemplation does man finally find himself and his own meaning, because only in this contemplation does he begin to find the meaning of God. But the author of the book points to what he describes as a "cloud of unknowing" which stands between us and God, and through which human knowing cannot penetrate. He writes:

> Try to understand this point. Rational creatures such as men and angels possess two principal faculties, a knowing power and a loving power. No one can fully comprehend the uncreated God with his knowledge; but each one, in a different way, can grasp him fully through love. Truly this is the unending miracle of love: that one loving person, through his love, can embrace God, whose being fills and transcends the entire creation. And this marvelous work of love goes on forever, for he whom we love is eternal. Whoever has the grace to appreciate the truth of what I am saying, let him take my words to heart, for to experience this love is the joy of eternal life while to lose it is eternal torment.[4]

While knowledge can lead us in the direction of God, knowledge in and of itself is never able to draw us into fullness of union with Him. In fact, it would seem that human knowledge *alone* can actually prevent us from union with God. Only when that knowledge coexists with and is transposed in love can one achieve union with God.

The gospel of Mark is a good place to take a look at this in the Scriptures. It is in Mark's gospel that there is the most emphasis on the "Messianic Secret"—by which is meant the fact that only gradually do Jesus' listeners come to understand his identity. In fact, Mark presents the teaching of Jesus in such a way as to emphasize that Jesus consciously hid his identity, as though it could not be known until people had been prepared for it. They expected a Messiah who would come in glory to restore the Kingdom and take away the power of the Romans. Jesus came a humble carpenter who established the Kingdom by submitting himself fully to the kingship of his Father. In the course of his teaching and actions the identity unfolds; indeed, it bursts forth and cannot be contained in secrecy. Over and over in this gospel the disciples are faced with the question of the identity of Jesus, and it seems that over and over again their idea of him remains too small and confining. He is a person of authority. He is a miracle worker. He is the Messiah. In the end it is only in the resurrection that they come to know that he is Son of God, and only then that they fully realize what it means to accept him as Messiah.

It is rather easy for us to look back and marvel at their inability to see the fullness of the truth. But could it ever have been easy for them to have seen that truth? The apostles were Jews and as Jews were the most convinced of monotheists. For them to accept even the concept that God could become man would have been unthinkable, perhaps blasphemous. Yet they did finally come to that conclusion and in the end were willing to face martyrdom for that faith. What accounted for the change? I do not think that we can attribute it to logical argument and intellectual proof. Many listened to Jesus. Many saw what he did. Yet many did not accept him, while the apostles finally did. What can account for the difference?

The apostles did not merely know *about* Jesus, they knew *him*. They saw, as did the Pharisees, that he cured the sick, that he raised the dead, that he forgave sins. The pharisees saw in this an insurmountable challenge. Who could forgive sins except God? Who could make such absolute demands to follow him, except God? They rejected what he said and did, because for them he could not possibly be God. The disciples, on the other hand, with all their bumbling and fumbling came to accept. Yet they must also have faced that same apparently insurmountable obstacle. The difference, I think, is in the fact that they knew *him* and in knowing him they came to love him. They saw not only that he performed miracles and made absolute demands, but also that he was *good*. What their minds could not grasp, their hearts could and did. Their decision to accept him in faith was, perhaps, not fully logical. On the other hand, it was not illogical. It was what I would call translogical. It took them past the limits of logic. Their point of view had opened their eyes.

Jesus had been for them not merely a teacher, but in his life and works he had proclaimed that the Kingdom was at hand, and in their union with him in love they had entered into that Kingdom. Their love for him had drawn them into the submission of their lives to the Father. It is important to note that Jesus did teach and that the disciples did learn. But it is, perhaps, even more important to note that he did not *merely* teach and they did not *merely* learn. He proclaimed and he called, and they heard and followed. What emerged was not simply new knowledge but an act of the full faith of total obedience. The limits of knowledge had been surpassed by a love which grasped the reality of God's presence. In the transposition of love, the knowledge itself was now seen from above and brought to life.

Within the Church, the theologian studies and teaches others. He attempts to devote his life to grasping some insight into the truth. But even the theologian must constantly remember that God is not to be found in knowledge alone. God is not to be captured by ideas. God is not to be analyzed and brought into subjection by human endeavor. He is to be loved and we are to live in his love. Only in this way, ultimately, are the eyes of our faith opened. To attempt to see God from any other point of view is to fail to grasp the necessity of transposition. It is to try to explain the Higher from the viewpoint of the lower—an effort always doomed to failure.

The theologian, if he is to be a theologian within the Church, must love the Church, for it is there that he finds his contact with Christ. He must be willing to work in harmony with that Church and with those in authority within it. He must not let himself fall into the trap of thinking that he is in search of facts, and forget that he is really in service to the Truth. He must not forget that it is the function of the Church not only to teach but to proclaim and to call, and that this may entail a call that cannot be bounded by the limits of his own logic.

The work of the theologian is of little value if he does not allow it to enter into the transposition that can take place only in a living union with a living Church, the living Body of Christ. The theologian tends to analyze, to find the parts of the truth and study them. Only in the living Church can there also be synthesis as well as analysis, the drawing together of truth into a lived reality.

One of my favorite authors is George MacDonald (1824–1905) who had been a minister of the Church of Scotland and whose writings were of tremendous influence in the conversion of C.S. Lewis. In one of his sermons he considers the notion of the truth, and in the course of that sermon he says:

> Ask a man of mere science, what is the truth of a flower: he will pull it to pieces, show you its parts, explain how they minister each to the life of the flower; he will tell you what changes are wrought in it by scientific cultivation; where it lives originally, where it can live; the effects upon it of another climate; what part the insects bear in its varieties—and doubtless many more facts about it.

> Ask the poet what is the truth of the flower, and he will answer: "Why, the flower itself, the perfect flower, and what it cannot help saying to him who has ears to hear it." The truth of the flower is, not the facts about it, be they correct as ideal science itself, but the shining, glowing, gladdening, patient thing throned on its stalk—the compeller of smile and tear from the child and prophet.'

The function of the Church is not simply to analyze the truth, but to live that truth and, in its living and teaching, to exercise the pastoral mandate to feed the flock. It is there that all our intellectual endeavor finds its union with a teaching that is not only intellectual but pastoral. The two are interdependent, but in a transposed way. The intellectual analysis loses itself in its individual parts if it does not find its transposed life in the feeding of the flock. For the individual theologian, this can once more be characterized in terms of his point of view.

Let us listen once more to MacDonald when, further on in the same sermon, he writes:

> The highest truth to the intellect, the abstract truth, is the relation in which man stands to the Source of his being—his will to the Will whence it became a will, his love to the Love that kindled his power to love, his intellect to the Intellect that lighted his. If a man deal with these things only as things to be dealt with, as objects of thought, as ideas to be analyzed and arranged in their due order and right relation, he treats them as facts and not as truths, and is

no better, probably much the worse, for his converse with them, for he knows in a measure, and is false to all that is more worthy of his faithfulness.

But when the soul, or heart, or spirit, or what you please to call that which is the man himself and not his body, sooner or later becomes aware that he needs some one above him, whom to obey, in whom to rest, from whom to seek deliverance from what in himself is despicable, disappointing, unworthy even of his own interest; when he is aware of an opposition in him, what is not harmony; that while he hates it, there is yet present with him, and seeming to be himself, what sometimes he calls *the old Adam*, sometimes *the flesh*, sometimes *his lower nature*, sometimes *his evil self*; and sometimes recognizes as simply that part of his being where God is not; then indeed is the man in the region of truth, and beginning to come true in himself.[6]

All human beings must come to this realization that we are not autonomous, that we are not subject only to our own minds or to the perceptions of our own limited logic. All of us need to come to this realization of the need to seek one above us to obey. Every member of the Church, no matter what his task or office or function, needs to be aware of the totality of his need to respond in loving obedience to God. Only in this way are the eyes of our faith really opened. Only then can there be the real transposition with its realization that faith involves not only the acceptance of doctrine and our need to study that doctrine, but there is the need as well to accept in faith the pastoral concerns of the Church.

Do we look at the truth and attempt to make judgments about it from the viewpoint of knowledge alone? Or do we attempt instead to look from the viewpoint of the living love of the Body of Christ? It is only in our living union with the Body of Christ that we can ever hope to see with His eyes. Only then do we experience the final transposition. Only then do we see not only the impressive promontory of theological endeavor, but also that Special Face which alone gives it life and meaning. The point of view is essential.

Notes

[1]J.R.R. Tolkien, "On Fairy Stories," in *The Tolkien Reader,* Ballantine Books, New York, 1966, pp. 3–73.
[2]C.S. Lewis, "Transposition," in *The Weight of Glory,* Wm. B. Eerdmans Publishing Co., Grand Rapids, 1966.
[3]Lewis, *op.cit.,* pp. 20–21.
[4]*The Cloud of Unknowing,* newly edited by William Johnston, Image Books, 1973, p. 50.
[5]George MacDonald, *Creation in Christ,* edited by Rolland Hein, Harold B. Shaw Publishers, Wheaton, Illinois, 1976, pp. 145–146.
[6]*Ibid,* pp. 148–149.

Chapter 2

Saint Paul and the Church in Corinth

We have looked at the importance of a transposed point of view. We have seen its value in looking at cliffs, in grasping the meaning of a fairy tale, in seeing the unexpected, in living out our sacramental life and in touching the real depths of union with God in and through the life of the Church. There is a still greater depth to be attained, and we can begin the process of its attainment by examining Saint Paul's First Epistle to the Corinthians.[1] Paul's relationship to the people of Corinth seems to have been a mixture of frustration and affection. It was, in a special sense, *his* community. At the same time, it was composed overwhelmingly of converted pagans whose culture was not yet totally Christianized. Time after time, it would seem, Paul had to teach, instruct and reprimand. Yet it was in the course of this constant correspondence and visitation that there developed some of Paul's deepest insights into the reality of union in Christ. To arrive at our own understanding of this union as explained by Paul we must study this letter very carefully. This is not an easy task and so we must be prepared not only to look at what he wrote but also to meditate upon it and to study the context in which it was written. Let us begin, then, with something of the history of Corinth so that we may proceed to Paul's teaching and its effect on us.

The ancient and famous city of Corinth occupied a location that made its prosperity almost inevitable. It lay on the land routes between Northern Greece and the Peloponnese, and its position on the Isthmus of Corinth, between the port of Lechaeum to the west and Cenchreae to the east, gave it relatively easy access to two seas. Its fame was not simply for prosperity but for luxury. The luxury overflowed into a proverbial licentiousness that had made the term "Corinthian girl" a euphemism for prostitute.

In the year 146 BC Corinth had played a leading part in opposition to Roman domination, and L. Mummius, the Roman general, levelled it to the ground. A century later it was restored as a Roman colony by Julius Caesar and by 27 BC it had become the capital of the Roman province of Achaia and the home of the pro-consul. Its prosperity—and its unsavory reputation—were well established once more by the time of Paul.

Its population included Romans, Greeks, Easterners and a Jewish colony as well. The last mentioned gave its usual opening for the missionary activity of Paul, but the pagan nature of the city would have made it an unlikely place in which to expect to find a flourishing Christian community—and yet that is precisely what we do find at the time of the writing of Paul's letters. In fact, many of the problems that Paul addresses would clearly indicate that the Christians would have come to a large extent from among the pagans (even if the Acts of the Apostles did not exist to confirm this).

The sorts of problems that Paul is forced to deal with are, in a sense, typical of this sort of population and culture. One such problem would have been tied in with the religious movements that existed in the Empire. There were real longings among the pagans for a more stable and personalized sort of salvific religion. Christianity must have come, for many, as an answer to this desire. But there were other answers also, including the Mystery Rites which had attracted large and enthusiastic followings. Greek culture had given rise to philosophy, and various philosophies had become tied in with religious concepts. Teachers of philosophy with their own specific brands of more general philosophies attracted adherents. Once philosophy and religion were bonded together, it was inevitable, one would suppose, that knowledge, wisdom and salvation would all have been interrelated. In later stages of history, not very long after the formation of the New Testament, we find a variety of developed religious philosophies (oriented toward strongly cosmological explanations of salvation) which can be grouped under a general heading of Gnosticism.

Gnosticism focused on the knowledge (γνῶσις) of secrets (mysteries) which explained reality and gave the initiated the key to salvation—salvation being, in one form or another, escape from this time-bound world and entrance into the mysterious realm of the gods and demi-gods. Certain characteristic qualities of the various gnosticisms would include a strong dichotomy between matter and spirit, a disdain for the limited body, a desire for the untrammeled freedom of the soul or spirit, a search for knowledge of mediators between this world and the world of the divine, and an emphasis on the secrecy of the knowledge to which the adherent was initiated. One could readily imagine how easy it would have been for many to begin to look at Christianity within just this framework, and history confirms that this did indeed happen. At the time of Paul, however, there is no evidence to lead us to conclude that such clearly defined movements had yet come into existence. There is certainly evidence enough, on the other hand, to allow us with justification to speak of an incipient gnosticism. Tendencies in this direction among the pagan converts can be seen even in the present epistle.

That Corinth was a center of sexual immorality has already been indicated above. This was due to a number of factors. There was a famous temple of Aphrodite in the city, with its priestesses who functioned as sacral prostitutes. A number of sources refer to as many as one thousand such being in the temple at a time. Furthermore, there is the fact that Corinth was a seaport, and sailors (even those not noted for religious zeal) might still have been inclined to frequent this and the other temples. But there is also another factor to consider. The incipient gnosticism just referred to also could have entered into this picture, giving a quasi-religious or philosophical justification to sexual aberration. In fact, the basic tenets of the gnostic attitude could easily result in thoroughly opposed principles. there was the characteristic gnostic disdain for matter and for the body. Only the soul had any part to play in salvation. On the one hand, then, it was possible to argue that the body was evil, it was doomed, and it made no difference what one did with it. It could not be further corrupted, and so sexual activity made no difference at all. Anything was allowable. On the other hand, one could argue that the body was thoroughly corrupt, and that any catering to it would lead the soul itself into a depth of corruption. For this reason, all bodily activity, in so far as possible, should be avoided. Therefore, any sexual activity was tainted with evil and should be shunned. Gnostic tendencies, in other words, could lead to either rigorism or laxism—and we find Paul in this epistle having to address both extremes.

The varieties of philosophical outlook and instructors that were present in this culture would also have led to a certain rivalry of schools and teachers, even within the same general philosophy. This attitude, too, could easily be carried over into Christianity, and preachers could be treated as rival with small groups of adherents formed into factions while still all considering themselves Christian. Evidence of this appears also in the epistle, as Paul addresses the problem of factionalism right at the beginning of the letter.

We should recall also the fact that there were varieties of Judaeo-Christian missionaries moving throughout the same cities that Paul had visited. These too seem to have come into Corinth, although their presence is probably more clearly defined in the content of the Second Epistle to the Corinthians than it is in the one to which we are currently directing our attention. These may have included the sort of preachers who looked toward the other-worldly aspects of Christianity and who saw themselves as a select group called to contentment rather than suffering. One can imagine that there would possibly have been some affinity between these preachers and the beginnings of certain gnostic directions.

This may seem a rather lengthy introduction to our study of the epistle, but there is a purpose to it. We shall now be able to see some of Paul's comments in a context that helps to bring them to life for us, and we will be able to focus our attention on the letter itself without the need for explanatory excursions that could be as distracting as they might be helpful.

As in most of the letters of Saint Paul, the opening lines set a tone and indicate a theme. This time there is the invocation of Paul's apostolic authority and an emphasis on unity in Christ that points to the union of the Corinthians with each other and with other Christian communities as well. He writes:

> Paul, by the will of God called as an apostle of Jesus Christ, and our brother Sosthenes, to the church of God at Corinth, to those who are consecrated by union with Christ Jesus, and called as God's people, like all those anywhere who call on the name of Jesus Christ, their Lord as well as ours; God our Father and the Lord Jesus Christ bless you and give you peace.[2]

There is in this salutation a pointed emphasis on unity, and it is a unity which is more than the moral cohesion of a group which simply decides to bond together for some common purpose. The source of the unity is clearly something other than the decision of their own wills. This is evident in the fact that the union is with Christ Jesus, not simply with each other. But it is further reinforced by the constant use of the concept of *being called*. It is a union to which one is invited, not a union which one manufactures. Paul is *called* as an apostle. They are the "church of God at Corinth" and the word "church" (here meaning assembly, and not universal church as it will later come to mean) comes from a root meaning, "to call forth into assembly." They are *called* as God's people (literally, as saints). There is union with those who *call upon* the name of Jesus.

Paul's letters usually have a note of thanksgiving near the beginning and in this letter the usual thanksgiving is filled with the emphasis on union. He is thankful for the blessing God has given them *in Christ Jesus*. He says that "in every way they have been made rich *in him*, in power of expression and in capacity for knowledge." Literally, the text says that they have grown rich "in every word and in all knowledge." "Word" can have a variety of meanings in Greek, and to speak of being "rich in every word" could mean a richness in all sorts of speech. It might even be taken to mean richness in one's grasp of the word of God, the content of the revelation.[4] However, Paul's explanation of the preaching of the gospel in the following verses of this chapter would not seem to support the idea of richness as being eloquence in preaching. In view of what he will later say, he may, perhaps, be taken as referring to charismatic speech, perhaps the gift of tongues. But this, too, does not seem to fit so easily here and is taken up only later on. Instead, when, after the reference to word and knowledge, he adds: "Thus the testimony of

Christ [which Paul had given them in his preaching of the gospel] has been verified in you," it seems possible that he is appealing to their experience of union in Christ to validate what he is saying to them. In this context he may well mean that in Christ—indeed, only in Christ—can they express the reality which they have become. The knowledge in which they have been enriched is to *know him* and *not simply to know about him.* In fact, further on in the course of the first two chapters, he appeals very strongly to knowledge of the person of Christ and not simply knowledge of facts about him. In other words, in the present text he seems to be implying something like this: "If you look at your own experience in union with Christ, you will see that in him your whole life has become an expression of him and you have come to know him." He is certainly not telling them that they have been blessed with a gift for theology and homiletic eloquence. The expression of the reality is in the living of the new life.

The experience of living a new life in Christ, and in that life expressing the presence of Christ, must have been quite vivid for the people to whom he wrote. The city which surrounded them, with its pagan culture, must have made their lives stand out in sharp contrast from those of their neighbors and from what they had been before. Not only the spoken word, but their deeds and lives were able to proclaim and bear witness to a new reality which had overcome them. We might also note, as a sort of undercurrent, that what Paul is saying also runs counter to a gnostic sort of secret knowledge, since what is being verified in them belongs to all Christians, and not to some select few. It is made open to all who receive it. They are to have faith in God. "Faithful is the God by whom you have been *called* into *communion* with his son Jesus Christ our Lord."[5]

Immediately Paul moves into the practical reality of the first question to which he must address himself. He faces the question of factions among the Corinthians, and forcefully denounces them. "I urge you all, brothers, by the name of our Lord Jesus Christ, that you all agree in what you say and that there be no factions among you, but that you be in accord in mind and in opinion."[6] He does not speak as though he is necessarily addressing groups who are in real conflict with the gospel. Instead, he seems to address Christians who differ only enough to be giving a different cast to the same gospel. Chloe's people (about whom we know nothing but her name) had informed him of what was happening and, in the first few chapters, he seems to be responding to what they had told him. Various groups were speaking of themselves as followers of Paul or of Apollos or of Cephas or even of Christ. That Greek tendency to follow one philosopher or another, even within the same general school, seems to have begun to carry over into their Christianity. Precisely how each group identified itself with one or the other is not clear, nor need it concern us right now.[7]

Their attention is immediately forced back on to Christ. "Christ has been divided up! Was it Paul who was crucified for you? Or were you baptized in the name of Paul?" What Paul had done was to preach the good news—he even goes so far as to say that he didn't come to baptize them (others did that). But his statement that he preached the good news should not be taken as though it meant that he preached a doctrine and they accepted it. That would put the whole question right back into the realm of a philosophy. And so Paul must go on to explain what that preaching of the good news entailed. He begins to develop the awareness that the Christian is, in a sense, not an adherent of a teaching but is united with the Teacher. We are not saved by a doctrine of Christ but by a bond of union with him. We are saved in union with Christ crucified and risen, not by common adherence to a philosophy.

> For to those who are on the way to destruction, the story of the cross is nonsense, but to us who are to be saved, it means all the power of God . . . Where now is your philosopher? Your scribe? Your reasoner of today? Has not God made a fool of the world's wisdom?[8]

> For Jews insist upon miracles, and Greeks demand philosophy, but we proclaim a Christ who was crucified—an idea that is revolting to Jews and absurd to the heathen, but to those whom God called, whether they are Jews or Greeks, a Christ who is God's power and God's wisdom.[9]

It is not human wisdom which saves us, nor is it the fact that Christ worked wonders. Rather, it is Christ himself, in himself, in his dying and rising, who saves. Paul has set aside any notion of the wonder-working Messiah who will conquer the Roman power and so found the new Israel. He has also set aside the philosophical mode of salvation, which would have been dear to the gnostic currents.[10] There is no comparison possible between human wisdom and the wisdom of God, or between human strength and the strength of God. They are so radically incompatible with each other that Paul can say: "God's folly is beyond the wisdom of men, and God's weakness is beyond their strength."[11]

Running through these verses is a constant contrast between God and the world. For Paul the world, the cosmos, is viewed with a connotation of weakness and sinfulness. It is the world under the power of evil or the world as still unredeemed. He will constantly contrast the wisdom of the world with the foolishness of God, the strength of the world with the weakness of God. To speak of the wisdom or strength of the world is to speak in riddles, since both are deceptive. In the end, what seems wisdom to the world is destroyed by God's choice of the world's foolish things. God's choice of the world's weaklings brings its strength to shame. What is low and insignificant and seems to be without being at all, renders the world's realities null.[12]

Again Paul appeals to their experience. He asks that they consider what happened when God called them. They were not wise or influential or noble. In fact, it seems as though God purposely chose the weak and the low and the insignificant, so that there would be nothing for man to boast about before God.

Instead, we were saved, we became his children "who for us has been made by God to be wisdom and righteousness and holiness and redemption, so that, as it is written, 'Let the boaster boast in the Lord.' "[13]

The passage just cited by Paul is taken from the prophet Jeremiah. The full passage there reads:

> Let not the wise man boast of his wisdom, nor the strong man boast of his strength, nor the rich man boast of his riches! But if one must boast, let him boast of this, that he understands and knows me—how I, the Lord, am he who practices kindness, justice, and righteousness on the earth . . .[14]

Where Jeremiah uses the word "Yahweh" the Septuagint uses "Lord." In the passage we are examining Paul also uses "Lord," but the reference is clearly to boasting in our union with Jesus, who is Lord. Paul has transferred the sense of the text to Jesus, and so is treating Jesus as divine.

Paul does not call Jesus "God" but "Lord." At the same time, Father and Son have attributes which are identical. Thus, for example, notions from the Old Testament which clearly were in reference to God are now referred to Jesus. The prophetic Day of the Lord is now the Day of Jesus. This day on which God judges the world becomes the day on which the Christ judges the world.[15] The Christian is in the kingdom of God, but he awaits the coming of Jesus.[16] Jesus is man's Lord and deliverer and through him salvation comes—all of these are notions which in the Old Testament were considered divine.[17] In Jesus we must place full confidence.[18] Jesus is the one Son of God, sent into the world so that we may become *adopted* children.[19] God's word and good news are at the same time the word of Jesus, Lord and Messiah.[20] It is God who makes Christians love one another, yet it is also the Lord who does so.[21] The blessing of God and blessing of Jesus are spoken of interchangeably.[22] Finally, the good news is not a human affair, because it comes from a revelation of Jesus.[23] There is no need for us, at this point, to make a further excursus into considerations of the divinity of the Son or the doctrine of the Trinity. It was not until almost three hundred years after the writing of Paul's letters that the Church came to the point of explicit dogmatic formulation of the divinity of the Son. All we need say at this point is that the realities which Paul attempts to express in a slowly developing terminology are the sources of the doctrines later expressed—and again only gradually—throughout the early centuries of the Church's life.

As we now move on to look at the second chapter of the epistle, we would probably be well advised to attempt to put it into context. Paul is going to refer back to his first arrival among the Corinthians. He came to them at first just after he had preached in Athens.[24] The account in Acts pictures Paul's frustration at the idolatry of Athens. Paul held discussions at the synagogue and preached in the market place. Even some of the Epicurean and Stoic philosophers were willing to debate with him. Finally they took him to the Areopagus and asked him to explain what he was talking about. His words on this occasion, as recounted in Acts, are different from what he usually preached.

There was on the Areopagus, among its many altars, one dedicated to the "Unknown God." This was, in effect, a sort of Greek insurance policy. It was intended to give honor to any god or gods they might have inadvertently omitted from their pantheon—thus insuring that those gods would not be offended. Beginning with the altar to "the Unknown God," he speaks of God as creator, the God in whom we live and move and have our being. He points to Greek philosophy and poetry and is, at the end, received with mixed emotions. Some sneer; some are converted; the majority seem non-committal but polite. They invite him to return and do it again. His success was minimal. He had felt the hard work and utter frustration of a man who spends a day trying to drive a rubber nail into a brick wall. At the end both nail and wall are unchanged, and there is no penetration at all.

Paul left for Corinth, probably feeling a sense of failure, perhaps even becoming ill on the way. It is in this context that we should hear his next words:

> So when I came to you, brothers, I did not come and tell you the secret purpose of God in superior, philosophical language, for I resolved, while I was with you, to forget everything but Jesus Christ and his crucifixion. For my part, I came among you in weakness and with a great deal of fear and trembling, and my teaching and message were not put in plausible, philosophical language, but they were attended with convincing spiritual power, so that your faith might rest, not on human philosophy, but on the power of God.[25]

A more literal translation of the same text might be helpful in coming to a better understanding of its implications. I would offer the following:

> So in coming to you, brothers, I did not come as a person superior in speech and wisdom to proclaim to you the mystery of God. For I determined to know nothing among you except Jesus Christ and him crucified. And I, in sickness and in fear and in great trembling, was among you; and my word and my proclamation [were] not in skillful words of wisdom, but in demonstration of Spirit and power, so that your faith might not be in the wisdom of men but in the power of God.

Paul is clearly appealing to a shared experience, and asking the Corinthians to recall just what had taken place. He focused his attention on the crucified Jesus. Since to accept Jesus is to accept God, we can better understand the folly of the cross. The true wisdom of the cross is in the Christian's union with Jesus himself, whose sacrificial act was perfect obedience to the Father. The center of the Christian revelation is not simply a doctrine; it is a person. Paul has no need to speak

18

in terms of human wisdom and eloquence when he gives the good news of Christ. The truth of what he is saying should be evident to the Corinthians in the very fact of their own already existing faith. They should realize that their faith was not inspired by Paul's weakness as he came among them in fear and trembling, but by the power of God operating within them and in the actions of Paul.

There is, in a way, the hint of another question now emerging. If the revelation which Paul preaches is true, and if it can be accepted by the power of God working within man, then why do not all believe? Paul's response to this comes in the next few verses and goes very deeply indeed into a realization that can give a whole new depth of understanding of the reality of revelation. For the first time Paul begins to speak of something to which he will frequently refer later on. This is the concept expressed in the word, "Mystery."[26] In profane Greek the word is most often used in the plural to mean the religious rites of the cults.[27] In the Septuagint the term is used in various ways. It refers to the mystery cults and is also used simply to mean something which is kept secret.[28] In Daniel it is used to refer to the hidden meaning of dreams.[29] It is used on a few occasions to mean a plan not yet known, referring, however, to the plans of the king and to those of God.[30] In a sense, this last meaning is closest to the way in which Paul tends to use it.

Paul takes the concept of mystery, and begins to develop it in a new way. There is a sense of irony which comes through if the Corinthians are actually being attracted to the mystery cults. In this case, Paul presents them with *the* mystery—and its secrecy is clearly not derived from the abstruse language and presentation of its preacher. What they treat as mysteries are mere child's thoughts when compared with the reality which confronts them; and their actions reveal that they are still children.[31] The wisdom they seem so anxious to have is there, but let them learn how to have it. It is a wisdom which appears as folly to all but those who are of mature faith.[32] It is a wisdom not intelligible without faith. The real mystery is to be found unfolded or unfolding in the person of Jesus, and only in union with him do we come into contact with it. The story of the cross remains nonsense to those on the way to destruction, but to those who are to be saved it is all the power of God.[33]

The entrance into this mystery implies something deeper still. Before we can grasp the full implications of what Paul is about to say, we also have to have a grasp of some basic concepts that he is going to use. He will speak here and elsewhere of man in a mode different from that which we would ordinarily adopt. It is, in a sense, a threefold image of man, expressed in the words: Body (σῶμα), soul (ψυχή) and spirit (πνεῦμα).

When we speak of man as being composed of body and soul, we tend to think of two parts, two components—a material element and a spiritual element—which together form the whole person. We think of them as separable parts and, indeed, we envision death as the separation of the two. When Paul speaks of man as body, soul and spirit, he does not seem to imply the same image of separable parts. What he is offering, instead, is a threefold way of looking at man, rather than three component parts. If asked about the component parts of man, Paul might readily have agreed that they were body and soul (a notion accepted by the rabbis). Fitzmeyer writes:

> Paul does not really describe for us man *in se* but describes, rather, different relations of man vis-a-vis God. These terms, then, do not really designate parts of man but designate, rather, aspects of the whole man as seen from different perspectives.[34]

Paul uses a number of nouns which have corresponding adjectival forms in Greek. One of these pairs is "flesh" (σάρξ) and "fleshly" (σαρκίνος or σαρκικός). This word carries with it a connotation of sinfulness or mortality. It is flesh in the sense of man as a weak and sinful being. For the moment we may set aside this pair of words, since Paul is not so much concerned with it here.

When Paul speaks of man as "body" (σῶμα), he does not mean one part of man. He means the whole person, the self, who lives in this tangible world. He is, in a sense, a body as are all the other tangible things with which he has contact. The body is the living being, however, and corpses are not referred to as σώματα. When he speaks of man as "soul" (ψυχή), he means once again the whole man, but this time viewed as capable of knowing and loving—an aspect that takes us beyond the realm of body alone. When he speaks of man as "spirit" (πνεῦμα), there can be implication of something further still. Spirit seems sometimes to be almost equivalent to soul, or even simply to "self." But there is also a sense of the knowing and loving person now susceptible to a new relationship with God. It is indicative of a higher mode of man's life. Thus, when Paul speaks of the man as soul, it has about it a connotation of human knowing and loving, but only that. It is man bound in himself, man at his human level, his old self. When he speaks of man as spirit there is the same identification of person, but this time it is the man taken beyond himself and more into the realm of God. It is a life under the influence of God's Spirit. In other words, he is talking about three ways in which one can live, in which one can relate to God. This is noticeable in the fact that Paul will not say that man *has* a body or *has* a soul or *has* a spirit. Rather, man *is* body, he *is* soul, he *is* spirit.

There are, as I mentioned, adjectives which correspond to these nouns. Two of them are easily enough translated into English: Bodily (σωματικός) and spiritual (πνευματικός). The word which refers to the soul is not so readily put into English. In Greek it is ψυχικός and simply has no real English equivalent. Its closest cognate is "psychic," but this would certainly not convey its meaning. In some of the older translations of the Scriptures, the word "animal" was used, based on the adjective derived from the Latin word for soul, *anima*. In the translation that I am going to use, it is translated as "material." So keep in mind that when the text refers to the "material man" it means the person who lives at that level of soul, man as capable of knowing and loving in a human way—but not going beyond that. When the text speaks of the "spiritual man" it means the man living at that new level of knowing and loving under the influence of the Spirit—in some way, knowing and loving as God does. With this in mind, let us look at the passage in question.

He says that we have a wisdom which we communicate to others, but it can only be imparted when we are with people who have a mature faith.[35] It is God's own wisdom, for there are things "which no eye ever saw and no ear ever heard, and never occurred to the human mind, which God has provided for those who love him." It is this new reality, in the mind of God himself, which has been imparted to us in the Spirit. This reality is beyond the level of body and soul and grasped only at the level of spirit. It is a reality which can be touched by man only when he is somehow drawn into the life of God himself—drawn into the bond of union in the Lord Jesus.

> For what human being can understand a man's thoughts except the man's own spirit [self] within him? Just so no one understands the thoughts of God but the Spirit of God. But the Spirit we have received is not that of the world, but the spirit that comes from God, which we have to make us realize the blessings God has given us. These disclosures we impart, not in the set phrases of human philosophy, but in words the Spirit teaches, giving spiritual truth a spiritual form.[36]

But if we are to grasp this communication of the Spirit, then we must also be changed. Mere human knowing would not be enough. We must see with God's eyes. In order for that to happen, we must be so transformed that we are able to live a life which goes past the limits of our simple human knowing and loving. This human level of life is not something evil in and of itself, but it has limits which make it impossible for us to respond to God's love as he offers it to us in Christ. Even our initial response to God at this level depends on the power, the dynamism, of the Spirit—a power given to us as gift in the proclamation of Christ crucified. The material man operates at the level of the soul; the spiritual man operates at the level of the Spirit.

> A material man will not accept what the Spirit of God offers. It seems mere folly to him and he cannot understand it, because it takes spiritual insight to see its true value. But the spiritual man is alive to all true values, but his own true value no unspiritual man can see.[37]

There is here a curious combination of human freedom and divine grace. Without being spiritual, one cannot grasp what God reveals. One cannot enter into or live the mystery without the transforming action of God. We can, indeed, by choice refuse to yield to the good news. In that refusal to yield, we are left so far from God that we are incapable of knowing what the Spirit of God offers, incapable of knowing even our own true value. Only in the power of God's Spirit can we ever be what we are meant to be; and only in the bond of union with the Christ can we approach the power of the Spirit. There is a tremendously deep awareness of the fact that our entrance into relationship with the Father depends on our living in bonds of relationship with the Son and the Spirit. Obviously, for Paul this can be no mere "legal" relationship with God. It implies a lived reality.

Finally, after having said so strongly that no one knows the thoughts of God except God's own Spirit, Paul now says: "For who has ever known the Lord's thoughts, so that he can instruct him? But we share the thoughts of Christ!"[38] The word translated here as thoughts is really "mind" (νοῦς), and the passage is a quotation from Isaiah 40,13. Paul is using the Septuagint version, but in Hebrew the word used is "spirit" (Ruah).

He takes to task the Corinthians and their attitudes, and accuses them of even now being material and carnal enough not to understand. The very fact that they are foolish enough to consider themselves followers of one teacher or another is evidence enough of that reprehensible attitude.[39] We should note also that although Paul always presents salvation and the giving of the Spirit as a pure and simple gift of God, he is certainly blaming the Corinthians for not receiving it as they should have. God's Spirit within them makes them temples of God, but one is still capable of destroying this temple and thus destroying himself.[40] For those who accept, all things are theirs. One author writes:

> It is not the faithful who belong to the apostles, as they pretend with their factions, but the apostles, their servants rather than their rulers, who belong to them. And likewise everything else is at their service: the world, which can lead them to God; their life, which brings them gradually closer to him; death, which will consummate the union; the realities of the present life, which already contain the seeds of glory; and the future will complete it. Everything belongs to them, but they themselves belong to Christ, as he belongs to God; through union with Christ, not by division into factions, they will share in the gifts of God which "he has prepared for those who love him."[41]

Those who submit to God must also be prepared to suffer for it. The world will not understand them, since the world is not spiritual. They must expect to be out of place, just as the apostles were.[42] Once again this is based in the fact that the Christian is in reality different. His very being is simply different from that of the rest of the world.

The reality of the change which has occurred within them is also in danger because of the immorality of their lives. Note that Paul never accuses them of having ceased to be Christians, although he constantly warns them of the risks they run. The fact of their Christianity seems to be permanent, although not to live up to this fact is to their lasting disgrace. As one might have expected in a city

22

such as Corinth, much of their problem had to do with sexual immorality. There is in their midst a man living openly in incest, and they do nothing about it.[43] Some of them still consort with prostitutes.[44] They must clean out the old yeast entirely and become fresh dough, free from the old as they really are![45] One is easily reminded of what Jesus had said: "People do not put new wine into old wine-skins, or if they do, the skins burst, and the wine runs out and the skins are spoiled."[46] Christianity is not merely poured into the old container (whether Jew or pagan), but the container itself is renewed.

This "renewal" of the container means that we are in actuality made new, reborn, transformed. It is at this point that our earlier consideration of the concept of transposition can come to our assistance. We are drawn into a relationship with God that gives new meaning and a new dimension to all that is human. The "bodily" man loses nothing of his bodiliness, except its limitations. One transposition had already been accomplished by the fact that we are not only body but soul as well. Through the spirit, however, Paul is now saying that we are drawn into a still deeper transposition. The "spirit" takes up and transposes all that belongs to the "soul." Paul, of course, never uses the word "transposition," but the reality of which he speaks certainly is captured by that concept.

There is, within Paul's description of what happens to us, another reality that is being expressed. I do not wish to imply that what I am about to describe is part of the conscious thought of Saint Paul, but once more the reality of which he speaks can be further described as we make use of some later terminology. When Paul speaks of union in Jesus and describes the transforming power of the Spirit in our lives, he is talking about what later theology coined a word to express—the Trinity. The words to express the reality came more slowly than did the growing awareness of the reality itself. It is not until a century or more later that we find the Latin and Greek writers beginning to use the words *trinitas* or *trias* to express what the Church believes. Nor does early theology, for some time after the scriptural period, have clear definitions of such concepts as "nature" or "person." Nonetheless, the realities are already recognized and a good deal of the Church's theological effort in the first few centuries went into clarifying the formulation of its lived belief. In the next few paragraphs, I would like to take advantage of that additional clarity.

It is easy for us even now to miss the point of the doctrine of the Trinity. We speak of it as a mystery, and so it is. We profess our belief in it, but we do not always seem to have a grasp of what this mystery really means in our lives. The terms "nature" and "person" can become difficult to understand when we apply rigorous definitions. But the basic concepts are not too difficult to grasp. The nature of a thing answers the question, "*What* is this?" It can be asked about anything, from an aardvark to a zither. The question answered by the concept of person is, "*Who* is this?" Here the question makes no sense if we are talking about furniture or animals or plants. It can only be answered when we speak about thinking and loving beings. The Trinity is not a mathematical problem of deciding how one can equal three. Rather, it is the mystery of the response that we must give when we ask about God, "Who is this?" and "What is this?" The answers, respectively, are: "This is Father, Son and Holy Spirit," and, "This is God, the divinity."

How, in the most basic way, can we say something about the theology of the Trinity? It is the inner reality, the inner life, of God. Theologians have tried by analogy to offer some insight into this. What they have done for centuries is to look at this in terms of God's knowing and loving. The Father is God, a personal God. He knows himself as God and that self-knowledge is total, full, absolute, complete, personal. It is so real that it is itself the perfect representation of the Father. It is itself a person, eternally generated by the Father as his own self-knowledge. It is the Word of God—the person of the eternally begotten Son. Between Father and Son exists a single bond of mutual love. This one love is total, full, absolute, complete, personal. It is itself a person, the person of the Spirit. So within God there exists an eternal relationship of knowledge and love. God's knowledge of God is the Son. God's love of God is Spirit.

We are consecrated by union with Christ Jesus. In him we have grown rich in everything. We are God's children through union with Jesus. But he is God's only Son become man. When we ask about him, "What is this?" we must answer, "God and man." He has become one of us, and so in our relationship to him we are transformed. We are one by adoption with the Son of God. We are one with God's knowledge of himself. And he has sent us his Spirit. It is this Spirit we have received, making us spiritual persons, alive to all true values.

This means that in some way our knowing and loving have been drawn into union with the knowing and loving of God himself. Our knowledge and love participate in the life of God's knowledge and love for himself and for his whole creation. From that point on, when we know and love God and each other, it is also God knowing and loving himself and his creation in and through us. We are and we remain creatures, but we share in the life of God himself. This is the real depth of our unity with each other, too. In this life on earth we already share this new life in God. But we are also growing into it. At times we have hints of how full it really is. This is the experience to which Paul so often appeals. This is the reality of the transposition.

Our transformation is no mere image, no simple figure of speech. It is a real entrance into the life of God himself. What has happened to us is so astounding that our minds can hardly grasp it.

How does this transformation come about? Paul's explanation of it begins, oddly enough, within the context of his statements about sexual morality.[47] I referred earlier to the sexual attitudes of some of the Corinthians, and I would not want the reader to think that I did so on the ground that since this book had no violence to recommend it, I would introduce some sex instead. Rather, the fact that sexuality involves the body leads Paul to speak of our union in the Body of Christ. It is from this point of view that he deals with both laxism and rigorism.

24

His concern is clearly expressed: "The body is not meant for immorality, but for the service of the Lord, and the Lord is for the body to serve."[48] It is within this context that Paul first mentions the notion that will be evolved into the theology of the Body of Christ. Its development in the First Epistle to the Corinthians is occasioned by Paul's attack on sexual immorality and disunity. At the same time, it is an essential concept if we are to learn what Paul is really saying about our unity in Christ. His notions of body, Eucharist, Baptism, spirit and unity are all closely linked.

The oneness of the Christian with Christ had already been expressed in his earlier letters. Christians are called to share a glory which is properly that of Christ (II Thess 2,14). They have the Spirit of Christ by which they can call upon God as Father (Gal 4,6). Christ must be formed in them (Gal 4,19). By being baptized into union with Christ, they have put on Christ (Gal 3,26). It is the action of God in one's heart that inspires our will and actions (Phil 2,13). The goal of the Christian involves recognition that all else is unimportant as compared to our unity with Christ (Phil 3,9). We have been captured by Christ (Phil 3,12). It is the power of Christ which will make over our poor bodies to resemble his in glory (Phil 3,21). In the present letter, there is a new turn as Paul explains that we are one body with Christ (I Cor 6,12–20; 10,14–22; 11,17–12,31; 15,1).

If we consider the sources of Paul's explanation of Christian unity, we must certainly take into account the corresponding hellenic notions of societal unity as compared to unity "in one body."[49] One of Aesop's fables, concerning the body and its members, had been taken by pagan writers and applied to the unity of the social order. The notion of this unity seems to have been well enough known that it would be a matter of no surprise to the Corinthians if Paul should also use it. It would certainly not be unexpected when Paul tried to organize the use of charismatic gifts in the liturgical assembly. Yet Paul takes it much further than this. He transfers the whole notion from the realm of simple metaphor to the realm of mystical reality.

The body of Christ with which Paul presents us is not simply presented as a figure of speech. It is not used simply as a metaphor for community, as we might be tempted to understand it since we readily identify Body of Christ with Church. Perhaps the best place to begin with an explanation of this is in Paul's statements about sexual morality.[50] The body he is talking about in that context is clearly a physical body. It would seem that he is attacking their apparent disregard for corporeal reality by showing them that this has a definite place in God's plan for salvation. The body is meant for service of the Lord.[51] The person who commits sexual sins is using his body to dishonor God, and in this sense is giving himself far more completely to sin than does one who commits any other type of sin.[52] Implied in this outlook is, perhaps, the fact that prostitution in the world of the Corinthians had a religious significance about it, for the prostitutes were priestesses of the temple with whom sexual activity also implied union with the pagan god. There is a clear awareness of the importance of this sexual union, when Paul speaks of it as making the two one flesh.[53] It is evident that Paul is referring to actual physical bodies, but always with the implied notion of the body as not merely a physical entity without reference to the world of spirit. The body (as we have seen above) is the person considered in one particular aspect—his existence in this world of physical realities.

The body as real rather than metaphorical is also indicated when Paul tells them that their bodies are temples of the Holy Spirit who is within them, which they have received from God.[54] Here the *metaphor* of the temple is predicated upon the *reality* of the body. The Christian belongs completely to God and so must honor God with his body.[55] The body of man in these passages is clearly his real, physical body.

Allow me to emphasize at this point the sense in which we ought to understand the "body" of Christ. We should *not* understand it simply as a metaphor for the Church. It should be taken in the sense in which Paul has already used the notion of body: It refers to the person himself insofar as he is a being present in this concrete and tangible world. In other words, the bond of unity between ourselves and Christ is to be found in our common humanity. Here again, the notion of transposition can help our understanding. That humanity of Jesus is the humanity of the Son of God. In our union with him we are drawn into that relationship with the Father. The core of the relationship is *not* entrance into a corporate body but into union with the person of Jesus. It is only later on that the word "body" in Greek began to be used to mean a body of people. And once it did begin to be so used, it made perfect sense, of course, to speak of the whole church as the Body of Christ—the way in which the term is used in the phrase "Mystical Body of Christ." In that context the term has had a fruitful history in the teaching of the Church. For the moment, however, we must be very careful to realize that the union of which we are speaking here is not simply the moral unity of persons who happen to belong to the same group. It is the infinitely deeper union of persons united to each other simply because they are united with Christ. This same understanding of the Body of Christ recurs as Paul speaks of resurrection (I Cor 15), baptism in Christ (I Cor 12) and the Eucharist (I Cor 10–11).

It might be well, at this point, to summarize what we have seen. We have been incorporated into Christ, so that we are one body, one person, with him. Now when we say that in Christ we have grown rich in power of expression and capacity for knowledge, the meaning is much more real, because we now see that we have received the word and knowledge of Christ himself.[56] We can, in fact, say that the revelation of Christ comes to life in the Christian. When Paul says that his converts are the sign of the truthfulness of his preaching, he is speaking of the reality of the transformation which has already occurred in them by their reception of the good news. We proclaim a crucified Christ by the very fact of what we have become.[57] The true wisdom of God has become known in us because we are united with the crucified and risen Christ. It is only in this unity with Jesus that we are able to receive the Spirit of Jesus. Through the reception of the Spirit we are able to "understand" the mind of God.[58] The words of Paul's preaching have resulted in the Corinthians' reception of true spiritual power and not merely in communication of knowledge.[59]

There is far more implied here than a revelation which would consist simply in the communication of factual information. There is something far more dynamic involved in what Paul says. For him the good news is Jesus crucified; and this does not mean that we receive the news of Jesus' crucifixion and resurrection. It means that we receive the crucified and risen Christ himself. We receive not just a spoken word, but the living Word of God.

This dynamism of the word is evident in Paul's own life. By the favor of God, Paul is what he is.[60] His attitude to his own apostleship is reminiscent of that of Jeremiah to his office as prophet. Jeremiah could not stop his preaching because the word of God burned within him. Paul says: "As far as preaching the good news is concerned, that is nothing for me to boast of, for I cannot help doing it. For I am ruined if I do not preach."[61]

The dynamism of the word has its effect in each of us, but that effect is not simply an overwhelming power which rides roughshod over our freedom. In one way we might describe this in terms of our choice of a point of view. We can see the reality of the revelation from the viewpoint of the spiritual man or from the viewpoint of the material man. But the viewpoint of the spiritual man also implies a commitment that is far more than intellectual.

We have already seen that the material man does not see the value of the good news. Only the spiritual man is capable of judging it. This is because only the spiritual man shares the thoughts of Christ.[62] This is not far removed from the Old Testament concept of the "new heart," which God imparts. There is an internal element in our acceptance of God's self-giving, and without this internal change we cannot accept the good news. If we were to say that the internal aspect is sometimes missing because God does not impart it, then there could be no culpability involved in rejecting Christ. Yet if there is one point which stands out in Paul's life and work, it is this: The man who rejects Christ does so to his own blame and condemnation. This point could be developed at more length, but I mention it now to indicate in another way that revelation does not consist in the simple imparting of knowledge. The response to God is not limited to an intellectual acceptance of facts. It must be a response of love.[63] Regardless of our earthly value or of our knowledge or power, we are empty and meaningless without love. We might simply conclude that what Paul is speaking of is charity rather than faith (to use a later terminology). This response, however, would miss the reality which is expressed. One may respond to a fact with assent, but hardly with love. We respond to a person with love. The fact that love is involved hints at the freedom of our faith, but it also tells us that God's revelation is a presentation of his person and not just a recounting of facts about himself.

There is, of course, no doubt that revelation does indeed involve the communication of facts, even though it is not limited to this. But that communication is never properly accepted if it is accepted only intellectually and without the living love that gives it meaning. The acceptance in love, however, implies more than the acceptance of a theology. It also implies a living Church in which we find Christ present and through which we communicate with him and with each other. It implies a cooperative effort on the part of transformed human beings in grasping and transmitting a truth that is not only intellectual but vital, life-giving.

It might be possible to misunderstand some of the implications of what Paul has said about our union in Christ. One might be tempted, for example, to think that since all are united in Christ and all share his life, then each one of us is in exactly the same position when it comes to interpreting this revelation and spelling out its implications in the living of our lives. In fact, I suspect that this was actually in Paul's mind during the writing of this letter. What I mean is that he has so emphasized the reality of the union of each Christian with Christ that it would have been possible for the Corinthians then to say, "But does this not mean that each of us has this same union? Does it not mean that each of us is spiritual and knows with the knowledge of God? Does it not mean that we need no longer listen to Paul or to anyone else who comes among us to denounce our factions? Does it not mean that there is room for dissent, and that no one can really tell us what the resolution of that dissent is to be?" Paul actually addresses this sort of objection, and he does so by pointing once more to the meaning of union in the Body of Christ.

In chapters 11 through 14 Paul deals with the question of unity as it affects the assembly, particularly the liturgical assembly. He is concerned that even there they seem to have divided into parties and factions.[64] Here the questions that he addresses are, it would appear, partially doctrinal and partially disciplinary. Their internal divisions have led to a lack of appreciation for each other, and this is totally contrary to what the Eucharistic assembly ought really to mean.

In the twelfth chapter Paul begins to enter into a different sort of problem, although on the surface it would still seem to be a disciplinary matter. He begins by saying:

> About spiritual gifts, brothers, I do not want you to be misinformed. You know that when you were heathen you would stray off, as impulse directed, to idols that could not speak. Therefore, I must tell you that no one who is speaking under the influence of the Spirit of God ever says, "Curse Jesus!" and no one can say, "Jesus is Lord!" without being under the influence of the holy Spirit.[65]

The test of spiritual gifts is their conformity to the faith. The person who is inspired by the Spirit will confess the lordship of Jesus. In that bond of unity with him is the key to understanding much of what Paul is about to say, and we should keep in mind that the bond of unity with him is also the bond of unity with each other in the assembly, in the church.

28

Just as Paul had earlier dealt with unity in what we saw to be a trinitarian context, so too does he here approach the whole concept of spiritual gifts. This is made quite explicit as we read:

> Endowments vary, but the Spirit is the same, and forms of service vary, but it is the same Lord who is served, and activities vary, but God who produces them all in us all is the same. Each one is given his spiritual illumination for the common good.[66]

The gifts that he describes are all, in one way or another, gifts of service to others in the body. He speaks of a capacity to express knowledge, the gift of faith, the power to cure the sick, the working of wonders, inspiration in preaching, discernment of true from false spirits, the gift of tongues and the gift to explain what is spoken in tongues. Some of the gifts are of the sort that we would classify as extraordinary, while others seem more related to the teaching and administrative tasks of the church. In any case, Paul concludes, every gift is produced by one and the same Spirit and is apportioned to individuals by the will of the Spirit.

Having placed the source of all gifts in the internal life of the Trinity, and having established their unity in the Spirit of God, Paul now goes on to develop this unity within the framework of the body of Christ. In this passage he comes closer to the analogy of the pagan fable as he explains that each part has a function and that this function is never executed in isolation nor is the function of one part useless to all the rest. But it should be carefully noted that he also goes well beyond the limited scope of the fable. What he describes is not merely like a body, it is a body. Nor is it merely a moral unity of persons who happen to believe the same things. Instead, he says:

> For just as the body is one and yet has many parts, and all the parts of the body, many as they are, form one body, so it is with Christ. For we have all—Jews or Greeks, slaves or free men—been baptized in one spirit to form one body, and we have all been saturated with one Spirit. For the body does not consist of one part but of many.[67]

When Paul speaks of Christians as "parts" the word that he uses in Greek is μέλη, a word which means the organs of a body. His point is clearly and emphatically that there is a vital, living union. A union founded in Christ, but a union of interrelationship of the parts. It is not ever described merely as the conjunction of disparate gifts which happen to work together. Rather, it is always a matter of a living bond of unity which is such that each part must make the conscious effort to live in harmony with the others and serve them. This is, indeed, the reason for whatever gift of service that organ has been granted.

That such gifts are not only what we would see as "charismatic" or extraordinary, but that they are also administrative and functional in the daily running of the community is quite clear in the catalogue with which he ends this chapter.

Now you are Christ's body and individually parts of it. And God has placed people in the church, first as apostles, second as inspired preachers, third as teachers, then wonder workers; then come ability to cure the sick, helpfulness, administration, ecstatic speaking. Is everyone an apostle? Is everyone an inspired preacher? Is everyone a teacher? Is everyone a wonder worker? Is everyone able to cure the sick? Can everyone speak ecstatically? Can everyone explain what it means? But you must cultivate the higher endowments.[68]

It is at this point that Paul breaks forth into that magnificent praise of love which he places at the pinnacle of all the gifts that can be received. In fact, while one may have some or even only one of the gifts described above, everyone must have this gift of love if the other gifts are to mean anything. It is in love that the remaining gifts come to completion, and it is in love that the bearers of the gifts—the organs—are able to work together. Love inspires the recipient of any gift to put that gift at the disposal of others, and to see that it is an integral and organic part of the life of the whole body. The love of which Paul speaks is far more than a sort of humanitarianism. Nor is it simply a love which can be defined in the rather negative terms of "unselfishness." It is, rather, a love which is active, creative, outreaching. It is a love in which one yields himself to active service in the love of God. It is, in fact, the love of God himself into which our human love has been transposed and comes to share in the divine qualities. Paul says:

Even if I give away everything I own, and give myself up, but do it in pride, not love, it does me no good. Love is patient and kind. Love is not envious or boastful. It does not put on airs. It is not rude. It does not insist on its rights. It does not become angry. It is not resentful. It is not happy over injustice, it is only happy with truth. It will bear anything, believe anything, hope for anything, endure anything. Love will never die out.[69]

It is, I think, almost impossible to sound the depths of the love that Paul describes. It is not simply a surface sort of affair in which we learn to be polite to each other. It is not so much the passion of love as it is the action of love. It is a communion with the power of divine love, and as such it is something that we never fully exhaust. It is a love which inspires and transforms. It is a love which assumes into itself all the other gifts and makes them what they were meant to be. The gifts that God has given us are ours since he chose to give them. But even after receiving them we are human and are capable of misusing or even abusing them. The man who has a gift of intelligence and understanding can so easily distort that gift into a means to his own ends. He can use it to get his own way and to manipulate others to his own will. To do so would be a distortion of a gift and failure to use it for the good of others. The gift remains but it becomes a means of destruction and not a means of life for the body of Christ. It is like a diseased organ. Only when the gift is given life in love does it become what it was meant to be. Only then does God's love come to life in its function. This is, I think, an awesome responsibility that touches the life of each one of us.

That this is consistent with Paul's thought becomes evident as we move on to the next chapter of the epistle. Taking two of the gifts—the gift of preaching or prophecy and the gift of tongues or ecstatic speaking—Paul compares and contrasts them. The gift of tongues he sees as having its merits, especially as a manifestation of the power of God. The gift of preaching he sees as serving the purposes of instruction which draws others to Christ. These and the other gifts he sees as authentically coming from the Spirit, and of this he seems to have no doubt. Yet he also quite clearly sees a priority among the gifts insofar as they serve others. When Christians assemble each might be tempted to insist upon his own gifts to the exclusion of the others, and this is precisely one form of the kind of distortion that I was attempting to describe above. In fact—and, so far as I am concerned, somewhat surprisingly—he seems to submit the ones that we might think of as more charismatic to those that are the more prosaic. Both prophecy and tongues seem to be subjected to the gift of administration, insofar as the one who is in charge of the assembly must determine how the others are to be exercised. He says:

> Then what is the right course, brothers? When you meet together, suppose every one of you has a song, a teaching, a revelation, an ecstatic utterance, or an explanation of one; it must all be for the good of all. If there is any ecstatic speaking, let it be limited to two or three people at the most, and have one speak at a time and someone to explain what he says. But if there is no one to explain it, have him keep quiet in church, and talk to himself and to God. And let two or three who are inspired to preach speak, while the rest weigh what is said; and if anything is revealed to another who is seated, the one who is speaking must stop. For in this way you can all preach one after another, as you are inspired to, so that everyone may be instructed and stimulated, for the spirits of prophets will give way to prophets, for God is not a God of disorder but of peace.[70]

At the end of the first chapter of this book, I spoke of the need to recognize that we are not autonomous and are not subject only to our own minds or to the perceptions of our own limited logic. There is a need to see ourselves within the living Church and to be willing to look at ourselves with a transposed way of seeing. We must see reality (ourselves and our own ideas included) from the point of view of the Body of Christ. This is not merely a matter of conjecture, but is firmly founded in the writings of Saint Paul.

The work of theology and the theologian himself must always be seen within the context of the unity of the Body of Christ. This means also that the theologian must be ready and willing to submit himself to that Body, to the Church. This is not because he acts simply on the assumption that those with the gift of administration in the Church are more intelligent than he is, or that they can give better arguments than he can. The reason is, rather, that the theologian must see himself as having an organic relationship with the whole Body and with those who represent its governing authority. This is not simply a question of keeping a "club" from falling apart; it is a question of recognizing our own responsibility for exercising our gifts in living union with the love of God.

The members of the Church are human, and they can, in all honesty, find themselves in disagreement. The theologian may, at times, have a special responsibility to seek the development of new ideas in his research, but these must always be firmly founded within the living tradition of the Body of Christ. Those who exercise the gift of administration within the Church have a special duty to see to the preservation of that same tradition and so can be called upon to confront the theologian when what he says runs counter to that tradition. The response on the part of the theologian, if it is to be in accord with what Paul is telling us, is not the response of bitter argument or simple disobedience. It should be the response of one who places his gifts at the disposal of the Body of Christ and uses those gifts in the building up of that same Body. A response which seeks the support of others so as to oppose authority is not a response which builds. The true response must be that which comes from the force of the active and creative love of God—a love which is not resentful, not bitter, not impatient, not envious, not boastful, not rude and does not insist on its rights. Such a response can come only from the willingness to see with the eyes of Christ, to see from a point of view that is truly transposed.

This does not mean that one simply remains passive in every instance, nor does it mean that the theologian must refrain from thinking and developing a theology. On the other hand, it does mean that one must see his interaction with all offices in the Church as the mutual functioning of organic parts of the same whole and not as a clash of rivals from which one emerges as victor. When the parts of a body are in conflict with each other, there will ultimately be no victor.

Notes

[1] McKenzie, *Dictionary of the Bible*, Milwaukee, 1965, pp. 100–102,150; A. Richardson, *An Introduction to the Theology of the New Testament*, N.Y., 1958; F. Zorell, SJ, *Lexicon graecum Novi Testamenti*, Paris, 1961; J.A.T. Robinson, *The Body* (No. 5 of *Studies in Biblical Theology*), London, 1963; L. Cerfaux, *The Church in the Theology of Saint Paul*, N.Y., 1963; *The Interpreter's Bible*, Vol. X, N.Y., 1953; C. Peifer, OSB, *First Corinthians, Second Corinthians*, Collegeville, 1960; J. Cambier, "La premiere epitre aux Corinthiens," in *Introduction a la Bible*, pp. 416–436; A. Wickenhauser, *New Testament Introduction*, New York, 1963, pp. 381–390; Feine-Behm-Kummel, *Introduction to the New Testament*, New York, 1965, pp. 198–205; F.F. Bruce, *New Century Bible: 1 and 2 Corinthians*, Greenwood, S.C., 1971; R. Kugelman, CP, "The First Letter to the Corinthians," in *JBC*, pp. 254–275; W. Bauer, *A Greek-English Lexicon of the New Testament* (transs., W.F. Arndt and F.W. Gingrich), Chicago, 1957, 1979; M. Zerwick, *Analysis philologica Novi Testamenti graeci*, Rome, 1953; J.J. Gunther, *St. Paul's Opponents and their Backgrounds*, Leiden, Netherlands, 1973.

[2] I Cor 1,1–3.

[3] I Cor 1,4–9.

4Cf. Zerwick, *op cit.*, p. 363.

5I Cor 1,9.

6I Cor 1,10.

7Cf. I Cor 1,11-17. It is easy enough to see how the Corinthians might have gotten divided into factions allied to Paul or Apollos. It could have depended upon which had converted them or baptized them. Paul quickly eliminates baptism as the criterion. However, there are also factions related somehow to Cephas or Christ. So far as is known, Cephas (Peter) had never up to this point been in Corinth, so it could not have been his preaching there or his baptizing which caused the faction which bore his name. Perhaps there may have been some Judaeo-Christians who had come to Corinth claiming a relationship to Peter and invoking his authority for what they said. Some would conjecture that this may have been a group which did not demand circumcision (since Paul would certainly have considered them worse than a faction otherwise) but may have insisted on such things as dietary stipulations of the law. The faction referred to as that of Christ could have been those who saw themselves as the ultra-orthodox. Or it could have been a group with the gnostic tendencies noted in the text, who might have seen themselves as being past the level of the others. They were filled with the Spirit and had no more need for other preachers. If you consult the various commentaries, you will find a number of conjectured explanations.

8I Cor 1,18-20.

9I Cor 1,22-25.

10Does Paul's concern with knowledge in this epistle stem from the Corinthians' attraction to gnosticism? There certainly seems to be a problem about their attraction to knowledge. A. Richardson (*op.cit.*, p. 41) writes:

> The objection to speaking of Gnosticism in the first century A.D. is that we are in danger of hypostatizing certain rather ill-defined tendencies of thought and then speaking as if there were a religion or religious philosophy, called Gnosticism, which could be contrasted with Judaism or Christianity. There was, of course, no such thing; a thoughtful person could not have been converted to Gnosticism in the same way that he could have been to Judaism or Christianity; what he might have done would have been to become an initiate in one of the many mystery cults.

This observation should be kept in mind. Although there is still no gnosticism here in the sense of the later heretical sects, there may very well be the gnostic mystery-cult initiation. They may have tended to seek in Christianity the mysterious cosmological knowledge which the cults offered as the source of man's true liberation from mundane existence. Even if this is not precisely what they were thinking, Paul is certainly closing off such a course.

11I Cor 1,25.

12Cf. Kugelman, *op.cit.*, p. 257; I Cor 1,27-29.

13I Cor 1,30.

14Jer 9,23-24.

15I Thess 5,2: 1,10

16I Thess 1,2,10: 2,12,19; 3,13; 4,16,23; II Thess 1,5,7; 2,1-2; 2,8; 3,6,12; Gal 5,21.

17Jesus is Lord: I Thess 1,1; 1,3; 2,14; 2,19; 3,11-12; 4,3; 4,17; 5,9; II Thess 1,1-2; 1,7,12; Gal 1,3; 6,14. Jesus is our deliverer: I Thess 1,10. Salvation through Jesus: I Thess 5,9.

18I Thess 3,9; II Thess 3,3.

19I Thess 1,10; Gal 1,16; 2,10; 4,1-7.

20I Thess 2,2,8,13; cf. I Thess 1,8: II Thess 3,1; I Thess 3,2; II Thess 1,8; Gal 1,7.

21I Thess 3,12; 4,9.

22I Thess 1,1; 5,28; cf. I Thess 1,2,12; Gal 6,18.

23Gal 1,11-12.

24Cf. Acts 17,16-34.

25I Cor 2,1-5.

26Reading μυστήριον rather than μαρτύριον in I Cor 2,1, and finding the word without variant readings in I Cor 2,7. The word μυστήριον means "mystery" or "secret." It was also used to refer to the mystery rites which had become part of the Greek pagan culture. This *is not* the first time that the word appears in Paul's letters, for it is found in II Thess 2,7. However, it *is* the first time it appears with the meaning of a divine mystery or secret. In II Thess it referred to a "mystery of iniquity." It will be used by Paul in a positive sense in: I Cor 2,1,7; 4,1; 13,2; 14,2; 15,51; Rom 11,25; 16,25; Eph 1,9; 3,3,4,9; 5,32; 6,19; Col 1,26,27; 2,2; 4,3. The same word is found in I Tim 3,9,16; Mt 13,11; Mk 4,11; Lk 8,10; Apoc 1,20; 10,7; 17,5,7.

27Cf. J. McKenzie, *op.cit.*, p. 595.

28Wis 14,15,23; Sir 22,22; 27,16,17,21; II Mac 13,21.

29Dn 2,18-19; 2,27-30; 4,6.

30Tob 12,7; Judt 2,2.

33

³¹Seeing here the implications of I Cor 3,1–4.

³²I Cor 2,6: Cf. F. Zorell, SJ, *op.cit.*, τέλειος, col. 1308: "2) de personis: *homo matura aetate, corpore animoque plene evoluto* . . . : inde accepta imagine is dicitur *perfectus Christianus qui sive in fidei cognitione sive in morum Christiano dignorum integritate multum profecit ac maturit;* οι τέλειοι I C 2,6, sunt Christiani sapientiae sublimioris capaces, idonei ad percipienda ea quae sunt spiritus Dei, in Christiana cognitione ac virtute maturi . . ."

³³I Cor 1,18; 2,2.

³⁴Fitzmeyer in *JBC,* p. 820. Fitzmeyer's treatment of σῶμα, σάρξ, ψυχή, πνεῦμα, καρδία and νούς are found in the same place. For each he gives a number of scriptural references as examples.

³⁵Cf. I Cor 2,6–10.

³⁶I Cor 2,11–13.

³⁷I Cor 2,14–15.

³⁸I Cor 2,16.

³⁹I Cor 3,1–3: They are still σαρκίνοι and σαρκικοί.

⁴⁰I Cor 3,16–17.

⁴¹Peifer, *op.cit.,* p. 19. Cf. I Cor 3,22–23.

⁴²I Cor 4,9–13.

⁴³I Cor 5,1–6.

⁴⁴I Cor 6,15–16.

⁴⁵I Cor 5,7.

⁴⁶Mt 9,17; Mk 2,22; Lk 5,37–38.

⁴⁷Cf. I Cor 6.

⁴⁸I Cor 6,13.

⁴⁹J.A.T. Robinson, *op.cit.,* p. 59, n. 1, writes: "We have here a good illustration of how Paul uses his 'sources'. It has often been noticed that the imaginary discussion between members of the body in these verses bears obvious resemblance to a fable depicting a quarrel for supremacy between the parts of the body, which had wide currency in the ancient world. Lietzmann refers to the story as having been traced back as far as the twelfth century B.C. (*An die Korinther I and II, 3th Aufl.,* 62). It appears in its most accessible form in Livy II, 32,9–12, in the fable of Menius Agrippa, and is a particular favourite of stoic writers. Lietzmann notes this or similar ideas in Dionysius of Halicarnassus, Plutarch, Aurelius Victor, Valerius Maximus, Cicero, Seneca, Sextus Empiricus, Marcus Aurelius, and I Clement; to which should be added Xenephon (*Mem. II,* 3,18), Philo (*De Praem. et Poen.,* 19 (114); 20, (125); *De virt. 20* (103), and the Midrash on Pss 14,1 and 39,2 quoted by Strack-Billerbeck, *Kommentar zum Neuen Testament* on I Cor 12,12ff.

"The fable as it is related by Dionysius of Halicarnassus (*Antt. Rom.,* III, 1.5) is worth quoting in part. 'A commonwealth resembles a human body. For each of them is composite and consists of many parts; and no one of their parts either has the same function or performs the same service as the others. If now these parts of the human body should be endowed, each for itself, with perception and a voice of its own and a sedition should then arise among them, all of them uniting against the hands, that they ply the crafts, secure provisions, fight with enemies, and contribute many other advantages toward the common good; the shoulders, that they bear all the burdens; the mouth that it speaks; the head, that it sees and hears and comprehending the other senses, possesses all those by which the thing is preserved; and then all these should say to the belly, "An you, good creature, which of these things do you do? . . ." Then follows a defence of the belly, as sustaining all, though it seems to do nothing but take in; and the same argument is applied to the function of the senate within the commonwealth.

"Now, Paul may certainly have derived his language in I Cor 12 (though not necessarily elsewhere) from these or similar sources. But the differences should be carefully noted. (1) We are in these writers dealing simply with a simile ('A commonwealth resembles a human body'). 'For Paul, however, this is not merely a simile, but a mystical truth' (H. Lietzmann, *ib.,* 52; cf. J. Weiss, in Meyer's *Kommentar, I Kor.,* 302): the Church is the body of Christ. (2) Paul's point is not to demonstrate the need for unity among the members, nor to prove which is the greatest, but to show that the body must be made up of more than one person quite superfluous in the case of a commonwealth, most necessary in the case of an individual organism. The whole underlying conception is different."

⁵⁰I Cor 6,12–20.

⁵¹I Cor 6,13.

⁵²I Cor 6,18.

⁵³I Cor 6,16.

⁵⁴I Cor 6,19.

⁵⁵I Cor 6,20.

⁵⁶I Cor 1,5.

34

[57]I Cor 1,22.
[58]I Cor 2,8–15.
[59]I Cor 4,15–20; cf. 2,4–5.
[60]I Cor 15,10.
[61]I Cor 9,16; cf. Jer 20,9.
[62]I Cor 2,14–15.
[63]I Cor 13,1–13.
[64]I Cor 11,17–34.
[65]I Cor 12,1–13.
[66]I Cor 12,4–7.
[67]I Cor 12,11–14.
[68]I Cor 12,27–31.
[69]I Cor 13,3–7.
[70]I Cor 14,26–33.

Chapter 3

The Living Church

Somewhere in the dim, dark recesses of pre-history, an unknown genius had a truly novel idea. It occurred in an age when people had no need for health spas with their polished chrome machinery for body building, when the lifting of heavy weights was not a pastime designed to improve muscle tone so much as it was a necessity of life. It was a time when hardly anyone could have had a sedentary occupation and physical fitness was not prescribed by either doctors or movie stars or gurus, but was a basic prerequisite for living at all. It was an era when pumping iron was not in vogue, because iron had not yet been discovered. None-theless, someone did manage to invent one of the greatest labor saving devices of all time—the wheel! And it really caught on. As word spread, everyone began to use them, and we could hardly get along without them even now. From generation to generation it rolled its way through time, taking its place among humanity's great achievements and never needing to be re-invented.

It is this fact—that each generation need not invent it anew—which is my reason for discussing it now. I want to move on to consider some of the implica-tions of the elements developed in the preceding chapters. Saint Paul presented us with deep and abiding insight into the reality of life in union with Christ, the life of the Church. Our lives are drawn into a union with the life of a trinitarian God, a union which is beyond the power of our intellects to grasp fully and which is in some way attained to only by the intellect which lives within that unity of love, only by the mind transposed into newness of life.

The temptation I felt as I began this chapter was to attempt to establish and prove the fact of the Church as a community in union with Christ, a structured community with its varied parts—all of them essential to the life of each other. Such a study could go on to a length far beyond the boundaries of what I had originally hoped to express. Then I was struck by the obvious. I need not re-invent the wheel. I need not attempt to establish, as though for the first time, a thing which was established long before ever I came on the scene. Without re-inventing the wheel I could, on the other hand, extol its functional character, its simplicity of design, its necessity to modern civilization, the varied forms to which its basic structure is susceptible. Anyone who had used a wheel would know what I meant. None of what I had to say would have made the wheel new, but it could inspire a new appreciation of the old. I can, in a way, accomplish something of the same goal with the subject at hand.

What I want to do, then, is to look at the past, to recall the way in which the Church has lived its life in union with Christ.[1] In the framework of its lived history we find certain extraordinary individuals who have been capable both of living and expressing that reality. We find exemplified in them a sense of the depth of what it means to be members of that Body of Christ. We discover in them also a capacity to reflect on and express the teaching of the Church. The most outstanding of them were able to see their faith and their theology as living expressions of union with God in the Church and were able to capture this in words. They saw the reality of the Church as Body of Christ and as visible, structured community. They recognized that their own union with him meant that they lived also in union with the members, including the leaders, of the Church.

As a child grows there is a process of self-discovery that is a wonder for his parents and, I am sure, an even greater wonder for the child to whom all is new and fresh. The childhood of the Church was just such a time of discovery. Its new life in union with Christ had begun and there still lay ahead of it the disclosure of what this was to mean. It learned who it was in the love of a saving and protecting God, somewhat as the child finds its identity in the warmth of the procreative love of its parents. But the child also learns about itself in moments of conflict and in the experience of being thrust into a world which can be cold and cruel. The infancy of the Church was no different. It faced misunderstanding, hostility and rejection. The whole Church and its members came to know that living in union with Christ meant not only the reception of the gift of rising to new life. It also involved the process of suffering and death—that cup from which Jesus drank and which James and John had been so unwittingly willing to share.

A few years of persecution by the Jews and a far more protracted persecution by the pagans soon taught the infant Church what its new life really meant.

Christians began to experience what Saint Paul knew when he said, "I live now, not I, but Christ lives in me." What we examined earlier by means of the concept of transposition was for them (as it must be for us) a lived and often painful reality. To find our lives transposed into the life of Christ is a fact which takes us far beyond ourselves and puts us into confrontation with a world which does not see with the same eyes and can make no sense of what the Christian claims.

The early, post-apostolic period of the Church's life was a time of trial about which we know less than we would like to. Only later, when the Church found a time of relative peace, was there the full flowering of an abundant Christian literature. From this earliest age there remain few documents and fragments. What does remain, however, is most enlightening. There is in this earliest period one individual who stands out and captures the imagination of later ages. About him we know, in fact, but little. His name was Ignatius and he was bishop of the city of Antioch. Sometime during the first few years of the Second Century—perhaps about 110 AD?—he was arrested and taken to Rome to die in the arena. On the way there—a slow passage during which he stopped at a number of cities where there were Christians—he wrote seven letters. One was to Polycarp of Smyrna, one was sent ahead to Rome, and five were to various churches in the East.

One of the problems faced by the Church in its early days was the heresy called Docetism, the error of those who could not believe that the Son of God had truly become man. Flesh was too corrupt for God ever to have assumed it. Salvation was totally other-worldly, an escape of the soul from its fleshly prison. The reality of our union with God was somewhere deep within and could not actually involve this earthly life. But Ignatius saw things differently. To the Trallians he wrote:

> Turn a deaf ear, then, when anyone speaks to you apart from Jesus Christ, who was of the family of David and of Mary, who was truly born, who ate and drank, was truly persecuted under Pontius Pilate, was truly crucified and died in the sight of those in heaven and on earth and in the underworld, who also was truly raised from the dead when His Father raised Him up. And in the same manner His Father will raise us up in Christ Jesus, if we believe in Him without whom we have no hope.[2]

Jesus was a real man and died a real death. In union with him we are to do the same. Ignatius rejoiced to be able to share in that death, and his letter to the Romans was a plea that they not try to interfere with what was about to happen. Ignatius' own fleshly death was part of the process of his salvation. To the Romans he wrote:

> I am writing to all the Churches and I enjoin all, that I am dying willingly for God's sake, if only you do not prevent it. I beg of you,

do not do me an untimely kindness. Allow me to be eaten by the beasts, which are my way of reaching God. I am God's wheat, and I am to be ground by the teeth of wild beasts, so that I may become the pure bread of Christ.[3]

The final act of martyrdom is not an isolated event in which one finds union with Christ. That union had long since begun and was reflected in the reality of the choice made by the Christian to live within the visible and structured community which is the Church. Martyrdom begins in the daily choice of yielding oneself to the needs of others in the humdrum frictions of normal life. To those in Philadelphia he wrote:

I cried out while I was in your midst, I spoke with a loud voice, the voice of God: "Give heed to the bishop and the presbytery and the deacons." Some suspected me of saying this because I had previous knowledge of the division which certain persons had caused; but He for whom I am in chains is my witness that I had no knowledge of this from any human being. It is the Spirit who kept preaching these words: "Do nothing without the bishop, keep your body as the temple of God, love unity, flee from divisions, be imitators of Jesus Christ, as He was imitator of the Father.[4]

The unity is more than internal and far from minimal. It is a doctrinal unity, to be sure, but not just the legalism of doctrinal acceptance. It is to accept the Church as the community in which Christ resides and is alive. One cannot be satisfied with saying, "Tell me what the defined doctrines are and that I will accept. The rest is a matter of opinion." One must, instead, live the life of the Church in which Christ is to be found. Again to the Philadelphians he says:

I beseech you, therefore, do nothing in a spirit of division, but act according to Christian teaching. Indeed, I heard some men saying: "If I do not find it in the official records in the gospel I do not believe." And when I made answer to them, "It is written!" they replied, "That is the point at issue." But to me, the official record is Jesus Christ; the inviolable record is His cross, His death, and His resurrection, and the faith which He brings about:—in these I desire to be justified by your prayers.[5]

These letters were written when many who had known the apostles were still alive. This is one of the reasons why they are so valuable to us. What Ignatius says of the position and authority of the bishops is presented as a truth already accepted and well known by all to whom he writes. There is no argument or attempt to prove; there is only the statement of fact and his readers are called upon to live up to what this implies. Indeed, unity with the bishop is merged into baptismal and Eucharistic unity as well. What appears on the surface as unity of discipline is intimately related to unity of doctrine and worship. To the Smyrnians he writes:

> All of you must be obedient to the bishop as Jesus Christ is to the Father, and to the board of elders as to the apostles; and let us revere the deacons as the commandment of God. Apart from the bishop let no one carry out those actions which belong to the Church. Let that Eucharist be considered valid which is conducted under the bishop, or under him to whom the bishop has granted the authority. Where the bishop is, there let the assembly be, just as where Christ Jesus is, there is the universal church (ἡ καθολικὴ ἐκκλησία). Without the bishop it is lawful neither to baptize nor to celebrate the *agape;* but whatever he has approved, this is also pleasing to God, so that all that is done will be confirmed and valid.[6]

Ignatius went to Rome, and there he died a martyr—a witness. That to which he bore witness was the presence of Christ within himself. His life, his letters, his concern for the Church—these are all part of the testimony. They testify not only to his own sanctity but also to the life of the early Church and its growth in self-awareness. Unity is the keynote. We are one in Christ. This means, as it did for Paul, a living unity expressed in the sacramental life of the Church, in its teaching, in its faith. It is a unity of life. For Ignatius it is a wholehearted unity, not a kind of begrudging acquiesence to the minimum. It is a unity in which one places oneself at the service of the Church so as to be in service to God. This demands much of the individual and is part of the process of martyrdom. Ignatius was no Pollyanna, thinking that such community was easy and came without thought or self-sacrifice. Indeed, the fact that he found it necessary to address the topic over and over again tells us that he clearly recognized the inherent difficulties. But he lived it and exhorted others to do the same. Only because Ignatius' life had been transposed in union with Christ could he say what he said and do what he did. He saw reality through the eyes of Christ.

In view of the last chapter, you may be asking, "Whatever became of good old Gnosticism?" Well, it was still around. It continued to attract the unwary, the falsely unworldly and various seekers of secret sagacity. One of those who opposed its claims was Irenaeus of Lyons, about whom we know more than we do about Ignatius, but still not a great deal. He had come from Asia Minor, probably from Smyrna since he says that he had known Polycarp. Our first glimpse of him is in 177 AD as an elder of the Church of Lyons who was sent as an emissary to Rome. Upon his return he succeeded Photinus as bishop. What was an Asian doing as bishop in Gaul? Your guess is as good as mine. In any case, his background puts him in a unique position to bear witness to the life of the Church in both East and West.

He wrote a carefully presented rejection of gnosticism, a book called *An Investigation and Rebuttal of Falsely So-called Knowledge,* known more familiarly by the shorter title of *Adversus haereses.* One of his major themes is what he calls "recapitulation" (ἀνακεΦαλαίωσις in Greek). By this he means the drawing together of all things into Christ. It is an all encompassing idea and does not by any means refer only to the coming together of the world with Christ at the end of time. It is, for Irenaeus, a way to describe God's plan of salvation. That plan which had been interrupted by the sin of Adam was now taken up and restored in Christ in such a way that the power of Christ reaches back into the past as well as forward into the future. The evil that for so long held sway was now undone and Christ was the new Adam, the inaugurator of the new creation. At the focal point of this recapitulation is the Church, whose head is Christ, and in the Church will be carried out the work of restoration. It is a powerful and beautiful image of what the Church, the Body of Christ, is meant to be.

Redemption reaches us through the Church and its sacraments, but entrance into the Church implies a doctrinal content as well. Irenaeus insists that this teaching of faith is passed on in the Church by means of a tradition which is tied to apostolic succession in the office of the bishops. He says:

> And so the tradition of the apostles manifest in the whole world can be seen in every church by all who might wish to see the truth; and we are able to list those who were appointed bishops by the apostles and their successors right down to ourselves, and they have never taught nor known such things as these people [i.e., the gnostics] rave about. If, indeed, the apostles had known such profound mysteries which they taught secretly and apart from the rest, they would most certainly have handed them on to those to whom they had also given over the churches . . .[7]

Unity with the bishop is every bit as important for Irenaeus as it had been for Ignatius, and for both it implies what we may only describe as the obedience of faith. Note that Irenaeus says he can enumerate the successions of the various bishops. In view of his residence in both East and West this was certainly no idle claim and he makes quite a point of it, for attached to the office of bishop is the charism of teaching the truth. Irenaeus writes:

> It is necessary to obey those who are elders in the church, those who have succession from the apostles, as we have shown; those who, together with succession in the episcopate, have received the sure charism of truth according to the will of the Father; we must hold suspect those others who stand apart from the main succession and have their gathering in any place.[8]

So does he ever get around to giving us those lists? Well, not exactly. Even though he had the information to compile them, he was realistic enough to know that his readers would be bored to tears in perusing them. Instead, he finds it sufficient to compile a list of the bishops of Rome, and his reason for choosing that Church is its special importance. He writes:

> But since it would be quite tedious in a book of this sort to list the successions of all the churches, we will refute all of those who in any way (whether for their own pleasure of vainglory, or through blindness or bad will) gather together illicitly, by pointing out the apostolic tradition and faith announced to men which has come down to us through the succession of bishops in that most eminent and ancient and well known church founded and established in Rome by the two most glorious apostles, Peter and Paul. For it is necessary that all churches (that is, the faithful in all places) agree with this church by reason of its more efficient leadership, for in it that which is the apostolic tradition has always been preserved by those of all places.[9]

Irenaeus sees salvation completely in union with Christ, a process of recapitulation by which we are drawn back into the unity lost in the sin of Adam. He sees the Church as the place where this occurs, and he sees the bishops as the visible sign of its unity. The tradition embodied in the bishops of the various churches is in some way summed up in the leadership of the church of Rome. He does not present us with a theory about Roman primacy, but offers, instead, a simple statement of fact. Rome's position is unique and that position is clearly tied in with the foundational notion of our unity in Christ. This is all seen, once more, from a point of view in which unity in Christ gives us the eyes of faith through which all else makes sense. As in the letters of Ignatius, so here too we are dealing with a description of a living Church and not merely with a tentative theory of ecclesiology.

When Irenaeus lists the Roman bishops, he begins with Peter. The fourth in the list is Clement, through whom we find evidence not only of the unity of the bishops among themselves, but also the special place of Rome. Clement wrote a letter in 96 AD, in fact the oldest Christian writing apart from the Scriptures themselves. He wrote to Corinth and he seems to have addressed, in a sense, the same problems of factionalism that Paul had attempted to put to rest. That church seems to have been governed by a group of bishops instead of just one. Some of them had been thrown out of office, and Clement writes in no uncertain terms that this was an illegitimate act. Never does he apologize to the Corinthians for "interfering" in their internal matters. The only apology he offers is that he had not been able to intervene sooner! Clement, who had quite probably known Peter and who was writing only about 60 years after the death of Jesus and 30 years after the deaths of Peter and Paul, speaks clearly and definitely about apostolic succession and its importance in the church of Christ. Poor Corinth! It seems a shame that they had so many problems, and yet they were the recipients of so many significant letters that we should be grateful to them.[10]

There are in these early centuries so many who deserve our attention, but there is simply no time to look at all of them. The life of the Church went on, nourished on the blood of martyrs, enlightened by the grace-filled minds of its writers and united in its faith in the tradition handed down through succession. Each generation inherited the benefits of those which had preceded and that once tiny community grew and spread so that it touched every part of the vast Roman Empire. Its touch transformed some and was violently rejected by others. Through it all the Body of Christ was alive and well.

In the Third Century, in Egypt, one of the leading lights of the Church's growing self-awareness was to be found in the person of Origen. He died in 253 near the age of seventy, almost but not quite a martyr. The desire to live and die for Christ he had inherited from his Christian parents. In 202, when he was seventeen, his father was martyred and Origen had tried to join him. All that prevented it was the fact—almost comical—that his mother hid all his clothes! Ambition for martyrdom was overpowered by modesty.

He was brilliant and was only eighteen when Demetrius, bishop of Alexandria, appointed him head of that city's famous catechetical school. It was also about this time that his zeal led him to take literally the statement in Matthew 19,12, that some have made themselves eunuchs for the kingdom of heaven. He had himself emasculated. Later in life he became famous for his allegorical rather than literal interpretation of the Scriptures—but it was too late then.

Origen was one of the most prolific writers of the early Church. He had patrons who supplied him with stenographers to take down what he said. As a result he produced thousands of volumes. His fame spread and, in 216, while in Palestine he was asked by the bishops of the area to preach. He did so, and thus ran afoul of his own bishop. Origen was not a priest and so, said his bishop, he should not have preached. About 230 he went again to Palestine and this time was ordained while there so that he could preach. Again he found himself in conflict with his bishop. As his subject he should have been ordained by him. Furthermore, Demetrius considered the ordination invalid because Origen had been castrated. In 232 Origen returned to Alexandria, after Demetrius had died and been succeeded by Heraclas, a former student of Origen. Any hope he might have had that Heraclas would treat him differently soon vanished when the new bishop repeated the old one's condemnations. Origen returned to Palestine and was encouraged by the bishop of Caesarea to open a new school there.

For almost twenty years more he continued his teaching and lived long enough to see the beginning of the first general persecution of the Church. In earlier ages persecution depended on the zeal and interests of local officials. Periods of martyrdom were local as well as intermittent. In 250 AD the Emperor Decius proclaimed the first wholesale persecution of Christians, and Origen was caught up in it. But his desire for martyrdom was not to be fulfilled. Eusebius, the ecclesiastical historian, later wrote a poignant account of his sufferings and the added cruelty of a judge who purposely would not kill him, although his death was finally attributable to the weakness in which his sufferings left him.

> The man's numerous letters contain both a true and accurate ac-
> count of the nature and extent of that which he endured for the
> word of Christ, punishments as he lay in iron and in the recesses of
> his dungeon; and how, when for many days his feet were stretched
> four spaces in that instrument of torture, the stocks, he bore with a
> stout heart threats of fire and everything else that was inflicted by
> his enemies; and the kind of issue he had thereof, the judge eagerly
> striving with all his might on no account to put him to death; and
> what sort of sayings he left behind him after this, sayings full of
> help for those who need uplifting.[11]

Even as he had been involved in controversy during his lifetime, so also was Origen the focal point of controversy after his death. He had been a pioneer in theology and so had pointed out new directions without having the time to follow them to their conclusions. Those who came after him often took his teachings and distorted them, claiming him as their source. This theology was grounded, to a large extent, in Platonism and this led also to errors that were indeed part of his work. His secretaries were overzealous in their publication of what he wrote, and so ideas were often spread before he had even a chance to refine them. He was a holy man, revered by many in the East as a saint, but often enough looked upon—especially after his death—as a proponent of problematic teaching.

Origen was especially captivated by the idea of Christian knowledge, the probing of the meaning of the faith. At the same time, his probing was neither random nor purely subjective. At the basis of any real Christian theology he saw the need for a rule of faith, a solid foundation of true Christian belief upon which the believer would build. He wrote:

> Since many, however, of those who profess to believe in Christ
> differ from each other, not only in small and trifling matters, but
> also on subjects of the highest importance, it seems on that ac-
> count necessary first of all to fix a definite limit and to lay down an
> unmistakable rule regarding each one of these, and then to pass on
> to the investigation of other points . . . as the teaching of the
> Church, transmitted in orderly succession from the apostles, and
> remaining in the Churches to the present day, is still preserved,
> that alone is to be accepted as truth which differs in no respect
> from ecclesiastical and apostolical tradition.[12]

Origen has articulated an essential insight into the intellectual progress of Christianity. There is a distinction between the speculation of the theologian and the data upon which that speculation is based. It is Origen's position that the truths of the faith are to be found in the Scriptures and in tradition coming from the apostles. This is what constitutes the rule of faith from which no orthodox Christian may deviate. This does not mean that the theologian is simply to repeat the doctrine as it is given to him. He must also attempt to explain it and to give reasons for it which are not always given in the tradition itself. The results of his speculation can give added depth to the facts of the faith, but they must always, in the last analysis, be in accord with that faith. The distinction between faith and theology begins to become clear.

> One should realize that the holy apostles while preaching the faith of Christ taught most clearly on those things which they believed necessary for all believers, even for those who were somewhat lazy about an inquiry into the divine knowledge, and the reasons for their statements they left to be searched out by those who deserved the highest gifts of the Spirit and who, through the Holy Spirit himself, received especially the gifts of language, wisdom and knowledge; on other matters they simply stated that they were so; how they were so or from what origin they did not say, actually so that the more enthusiastic of their successors who were lovers of wisdom might have an opportunity to show the fruit of their intelligence, namely those who prepared themselves to be worthy and capable of receiving wisdom.[13]

The gnostics, too, had emphasized the importance of knowledge, but their approach was much different than that of Origen. While they tended to view everything from the aspect of philosophical endeavor, Origen firmly maintained the necessity of a visible, structured Church within which one found the truth. He too speaks of the Church as the Body of Christ. His use of this term is not precisely the same as it is in the writings of Saint Paul, and he tends to draw an analogy between the soul and the presence of Christ in the Body of the Church. What is most important, however, is his insistence on the fact of a unified and living Church. He writes:

> We say that the Holy Scriptures declare the body of Christ, animated by the Son of God, to be the whole Church of God, and the members of this body—considered as a whole—to consist of those who are believers; since, as a soul vivifies and moves the body, which of itself has not the natural power of motion like a living being, so the Word, arousing and moving the whole body, the church, to befitting action, awakens, moreover, each individual member belonging to the Church, so that they do nothing apart from the Word.[14]

In Origen we see a man who, although he had some serious conflicts with those in authority in the Church, was ever faithful to it and was always ready to respond obediently to the successors of the apostles. In both his writings and his life he bears witness to what the Church believed about itself. In fact, his adherence to that Church is based on the deepest convictions of its necessity for union with Christ and salvation. He says:

> If anyone from among that people wishes to be saved, let him come to this house, that he may be able to attain to salvation, let him come to this house in which the blood of Christ is present as a sign of redemption . . . Therefore, let no one persuade himself, let no one deceive himself: outside this house, that is outside the church, no one is saved; for if anyone goes outside he becomes guilty of his own death.[15]

This man, so much aware of the internal and intellectual aspects of his Christian faith, was vividly aware also of the need for the visible Church. To live in union with Christ was not simply to acquiesce internally. It was equally essential to be united visibly with the living community.

That same Decian persecution responsible for the sufferings of Origen was having its effect in North Africa and in Rome itself. In Rome, Pope Fabian was put to death and it was almost a year before Cornelius was elected to replace him. In North Africa, in the city of Carthage, the threats of the persecutors had led the bishop, Cyprian, to flee the city for a safer place. This was in 250 AD when Cyprian was somewhere between forty and fifty years of age. He had been a bishop for only a year and a Christian for only four years more than that. When the persecution ended, Cyprian returned to his diocese and was faced with the aftermath of the imperial action. Many of the Christians had renounced the Church when their lives were threatened, and, now that the trouble was over (at least for a while) there were those who wished to return. Cyprian was forced to face the serious problem of penitential discipline for the fallen—the *lapsi* as they were called. His attitude was strict. The *lapsi* should be made to perform penance for the rest of their lives and be granted absolution only on their deathbeds. In Rome another man, named Novatian, was even more rigorous and thought that they could not be forgiven at all. Novatian, in what he saw as a superior orthodoxy, had himself consecrated bishop in opposition to Cornelius.

In the last few years of his life, Cyprian became involved in a controversy over receiving into the Church those who had been members of heretical groups and who had been baptized by adherents of those groups. Was their baptism a true sacrament? Or should they be baptized again upon conversion? In North Africa the tradition had been in favor of rebaptism. In Rome it had not. By the time that this became most controversial, Stephen had replaced Cornelius as bishop of Rome. It was in the midst of both these controversies that Cyprian wrote books and letters to explain the place of the bishops in the Church.

When Cornelius had been elected to replace Fabian, Cyprian expressed his happiness that the election had taken place. He wrote:

> Cornelius has been made bishop by the judgment of God and his Christ, by the witness of practically all of the clergy, by the vote of the body of people then present, by the college of elder priests and good men, since no one had been elected before him, when the place of Fabian, that is, when the place of Peter and the rank of the priestly throne, was left empty: once that place was occupied both by the will of God and confirmed by the consent of all of us, whoever still wanted to make himself the bishop would have to do so from outside, nor would one have ecclesiastical ordination who did not maintain the unity of the Church.[16]

In 252, when some of the members of the Church of Carthage disagreed vigorously with Cyprian on his attitude toward the *lapsi* and their reception back into the Church, they took their case to Rome. Cyprian wrote to Cornelius:

> Do the [heretics] dare to sail even to the throne of Peter and the principal church, from which priestly unity has arisen, to bring letters from schismatics and the profane, not stopping to think that these are the Romans whose faith was praised in the preaching of the Apostle, in whom treachery has no place?[17]

It is clear that he considered the bishop of Rome as the successor of Peter, and that he considered the place of the church of Rome as something special among the churches. Even while the See had been vacant, Cyprian had considered it necessary to write to Rome, reporting on incidents and seeking approval of his own actions. In the same letter to Cornelius quoted above, Cyprian also apologized for his tardiness in reporting to Rome on the consecration of a bishop, Fortunatus.

By 257 the baptismal controversy was well under way. Synods were held by Cyprian in Africa and Firmilian in Asia, and had agreed to the need for rebaptism. Stephen was informed of this, did not agree, and accused them all of innovation since this had never been the tradition in Rome. The correspondence between Firmilian and Cyprian reveals that they did not agree with Stephen and were shocked that he would allow any acceptance of a true sacramental life among the heretical sects. It is also evident in their correspondence that Stephen had based his claim to authority, at least in part, on his own Petrine succession. What Stephen was claiming was really jurisdictional authority over the other churches. It was not a new claim. We have, in fact, seen hints of it as early as 96 AD in the letter of Clement of Rome. Neither Cyprian nor Firmilian accepted this although they never disputed his claim to succession. We should also note, however, that the Church did come eventually to accept the position of Stephen on this matter.

It might appear that Cyprian simply discounted Roman jurisdiction, and this might be an acceptable interpretation of the whole affair, were it not for other documents written also by Cyprian. These reveal to us an ambiguity within the works of Cyprian himself, but they also tell us something else. The Church was still in process of growth. In fact, the Church will *always* be in process of growth because it is a living reality. From the earliest days the self-consciousness of the Church had included the essential place of its bishops. This we have already seen. From the earliest days there had been the special importance of Rome. This, too, we have seen. Nonetheless, the precise implications of the episcopal structure had, of necessity, to be worked out in time, within the framework of that same living church. Cyprian had become a participant in that process.

One of Cyprian's works is entitled *De unitate ecclesiae*, which means, *On the Unity of the Church*. There are, in fact, two versions of this work. One of them gives strong support to the Roman primacy, while the other does not. It had once been thought that Cyprian's work did not support primacy, but someone had interpolated passages into a second version. Opinion among critics then shifted to hold that Cyprian's earlier work did not support primacy and that he himself had later made the additions. The most common opinion right now is that Cyprian wrote both works. The earlier one is that which supports the primacy of Rome and the later, rewritten in the heat of the controversy over rebaptism, lacked those references. In the book he speaks of the Novatian schism in Rome and then says:

> Now there is no need for long discussion or argument, if one would only consider and carefully examine what I have said. We can find an easy support for our belief in a short summary of the truth; as the Lord said to Peter: I say to you that you are Peter and upon this rock I shall build my church, and the gates of hell shall not prevail against it. I will give you the keys of the kingdom of Heaven, and whatever you bind on earth shall be bound in Heaven, and whatever you loose on earth shall be loosed in Heaven . . .

It is at this point that the two texts diverge. The text which supports primacy reads this way:

> And similarly after his resurrection He says to him, "Feed my sheep." Upon him He builds his Church; to him he gives his sheep to feed; and although He gives all apostles equal power, He sets up one throne and by His authority ordains but one source and principle of unity. Assuredly the other apostles were the same as Peter, but to Peter was the primacy given, and thus was shown one Church and one chair. All indeed are pastors, but the unity of the flock comes from their being fed by the apostles in unanimous consent. If a man does not hold this unity under Peter, can he

believe that he has the faith? Whoever deserts the chair of Peter on whom the Church was founded, can he believe that he is in the Church?

It is this text which was removed from the second edition, and in its place we find the following:

It was upon one that He built his Church: indeed, after his resurrection, He gave them equal authority, saying: As the Father has sent me, even so I send you. Receive the Holy Spirit. If you forgive the sins of any, they are forgiven; if you retain the sins of any, they are retained. Yet that He might make clear their unity, He arranged for a source of this unity by his authority, beginning from one man. Certainly the other apostles were the same as Peter, endowed with equal partnership of dignity and of power, but [the Church's] beginning proceeds from a unity, that the Church of Christ might be shown to be one. The Holy Spirit also designates this one Church in the person of the Lord in the Song of Songs, saying: My dove, my perfect one, is one; she is the only one of her mother, chosen to her that bore her.

Whoever does not adhere to this unity of the Church, can he say he has the faith? Can he who strives against the Church and resists her trust that he is in the Church, when the blessed apostle Paul teaches the same doctrine, setting forth the sacrament of unity, when he says: There is one body and one spirit, one hope of your calling, one Lord, one faith, one baptism, one God.

Those of us who are bishops ought especially to hold this unity and defend it, for we preside in the Church, in order that we may also demonstrate the episcopate itself to be one and undivided. No one should deceive our brothers by falsehood; no one should corrupt the truth of the faith by malicious lies.

Both versions then come together again, and agree in the following passage:

The body of bishops is one, and each one who has a share in it possesses the whole. The Church is one, extended as it is far and wide among men by its increase in fruitfulness ... In her rich abundance she spreads her branches over the entire world; she pours forth abundant streams which flow far and wide, though her head and source is one, and she remains one mother, overflowing in the effects of her fecundity. Born from her womb, we are nursed by her milk, envigorated by her soul.

Christ's spouse cannot be defiled, for she is chaste and pure. She knows one home, and in holy purity she guards the sanctity of one couch. It is she that holds us safe for God, for she assigns to his kingdom the sons she has brought forth. Whoever is separated from the Church is wed to an adulteress and is separated from the promises made to the Church, whoever leaves Christ's Church will never attain to the rewards of Christ.[18]

The reverence of Cyprian for the Church and for episcopal succession is thoroughly evident. His attitude toward the bishop of Rome is ambivalent, and that ambivalence depends upon the stages of his life at which he considered the question. He does indeed recognize a primacy of Rome, but he seems to end up considering it a primacy of honor—the first among equals. Eventually that primacy was going to be recognized in the Church as a primacy of jurisdiction. In the heat of the arguments about rebaptism, Cyprian disputes this. It seems clear that we are witnessing a part of the process of the Church's own growing self-awareness. Cyprian focuses his attention on unity and clearly recognizes a unity of all local churches in one universal Church; but his primary concern in his discussions of the unity of the Church is to show that there must be an internal unity with the bishop in each church. This, together with the continued unity of the bishops among themselves, would be the guarantee of universal unity. The lack of clarity about primacy is accompanied by considerable clarity in regard to collegiality.

I say that his attitude changes as conditions of discussion change. This is clear in his letters. Both he and Firmilian, in their correspondence, complain about the statements of Pope Stephen in reference to rebaptism and they seem to cast doubt on his authority. On the other hand, in the controversies about Novatian, Cyprian's response was quite different. One of the Gallican bishops, Marcian, was in sympathy with Novatian and Stephen decided to remove him from his see. Not only did Cyprian not contest this action, he applauded it! He wrote:

> Therefore you ought to write a very complete letter to our co-bishops established in Gaul, lest they allow the obstinate and proud Marcian, the enemy of divine piety and fraternal salvation, to insult our college any further . . . Send letters to the province and to the people living in Arles, letters removing Marcian and putting another into his place and let that flock of Christ be gathered which until now, scattered about and wounded, is treated by him with contempt.[19]

The discussion could surely have gone on and, perhaps, come to some resolution between Stephen and Cyprian. This did not, in fact, happen. The Emperor Valerian, successor of Decius, renewed the general persecution and in 258 Cyprian was beheaded. He is revered as a saint and his writings remain to give us deeper insight into the life of the Church.

By the beginning of the Fourth Century, the Church and state had been reconciled in Constantine's Edict of Milan. For all practical purposes the time of persecution was at an end. With the exception of the reign of Julian (361–363, when an effort was made to reinstate paganism) the relationship of Church and state became closer—a situation which brought with it both advantages and disadvantages. Missionary activity expanded. The clergy, especially bishops, assumed a new role of leadership. Synods could be held with greater ease, leading eventually to the inauguration of the Ecumenical Council. At the same time, the state began to exert its influence in the realm of religion, attempting to control or influence even purely doctrinal matters. The blame for this should not be placed only on the state, since there were church leaders anxious to maintain their positions of influence at court by compromising their teaching. There were times when heroic individuals, such as Athanasius, must have felt that they were standing all alone as they called the Church back to its proper course and tradition. Constantine moved his capital to the East and then, after his death, the empire was split into two.

The Council of Nicaea in 325 met at the imperial summer palace near the capital and began the process of dealing with the Arian heresy. The council was considered "ecumenical" or worldwide, even though all the bishops of the world did not attend. There were, in fact, probably about 220 in attendance, including four bishops from the West and two papal legates. It was their desire to put into words the authentic faith of the Church in opposition to Arius' denial of the divinity of Christ. They did not accomplish their goal simply by reiterating the Scriptures. Indeed, the problem was to a large extent precisely a matter of the way in which one was to understand the Scriptures. What was needed was authentic interpretation. This the Council supplied, expressing the faith of the Church in a creed. That creed included the word "consubstantial" (ὁμοούιος was the Greek word). This term had not been used in the Scriptures, but it was judged to be an authentic expression of what the whole Church truly believed. The growing self-consciousness of the Church included its awareness of the ability to express itself, even in new words, when such words were a proper way to voice its faith. Again there were questions, and again development. The tradition, like the wheel, had not been reinvented, but it had begun to show itself capable of retaining its proper form while still emerging into a new age.

What was actually happening in the life of the Church was that, just as it had spread throughout the known world, so it also expanded in time. As it met and converted a variety of disparate cultures, so, too, would it live through the ages. Cyril of Jerusalem (313–386) sums it up in his *Catecheses,* when he describes what it means to him to say that the Church is "Catholic."

> [The church] is called catholic by reason of the fact that it is
> spread throughout the whole world, from one end to the other, and
> because universally and without omission it teaches all dogmas
> which ought to enter into the knowledge of men, whether about

visible or invisible, heavenly or earthly matters; then also because of the fact that it subjects the whole human race, princes and private citizens, learned and unlearned, to proper worship; and finally because it generally cures and heals every kind of sin which is committed through body and soul; and it also possesses every kind of virtue that can be named, in deeds and words and spiritual gifts of any kind.[20]

That word, "catholic," which Ignatius had been the first to use more than two centuries earlier, had remained as a description of the Church. No longer did it simply refer to the fact that it was spread through the world, but Cyril sees it as universal because it permeates the whole life of each of its members. In addition, this had even become its title. Cyril wrote:

And when you travel in cities, do not simply ask where the house of the Lord is, for other sects of impious men and heresies try to give dignity to their dens with the name of "houses of the Lord." And do not simply [ask] where the church is, but where the Catholic Church is; for this is the proper name of his holy [church] and mother of us all.[21]

Saint Basil (330–379) also lived in this age of the aftermath of Nicea, a time in which rival groups attempted to get the support of the emperor, and imperial opinions had all the stability of quicksand. Basil saw that the function of the Church was neither to propose philosophical arguments, nor to repeat the words of the Scriptures. Its life depended upon the continued living out of its tradition. He wrote:

Of the dogmas and proclamations preserved in the Church, some we have from a teaching passed on in writing, but others we receive as handed over to us in mystery from the tradition of the apostles, both of which make the same demand for our respect; and let no one contradict them, certainly no one who only from his own limited experience knows what the Church teaches. For if we attempt to reject as being of minor importance the customs which are not handed on in writing, we, through our imprudence, damage the gospel and indeed we reduce the preaching to the bare word . . .[22]

Basil's younger brother, Gregory of Nyssa (335–395), also proclaimed the value of this tradition:

Let him first show this, that the Church has believed in vain that this is truly the only begotten Son, not associated through adoption with a false Father, but according to nature through generation from him who is, not foreign to the nature of him who begets . . .

And let no one come chattering to me that even this, which is held
as our confession, needs to be confirmed and proved with reasons
and arguments; it suffices for the demonstration of our word that
we have a tradition coming to us from the fathers, as an inheri-
tance transmitted through succession from the apostles through
subsequent holy men.[23]

Saint Jerome was born about the year 347 in Stridon, and strident he could
be in his arguments with others. Unlike what pious legends say of so many of the
saints, he was born of a Christian family neither poor nor humble. He was given a
good education and was baptized at about the age of nineteen. He is a man of
contradictions. Deeply devoted to study and to the Scriptures, he was also irascible
and difficult to argue with. He saw enemies all about, and he was not always
unjustified in his fears. He was the secretary of Pope Damasus for a few years and
was even spoken of as his possible successor, but he decided to leave Rome when
people made unjustified accusations about his relationship with a group of noble
women whom he was instructing in the reading of the Scriptures. He spent the
last thirty-five years of his life in the Holy Land, where he completed his translation of the Bible into Latin. In controversy he was the epitome of polemical
overkill and preferred the elephant gun even to get rid of fleas. But he was also a
holy man, loyal to his friends and deeply loyal to the Church. He saw separation
from the Church as fatal, and felt that even schism, in the end, destroyed the truth
of doctrine.

> We make this distinction between heresy and schism: Heresy con-
> tains a perversion of dogma; schism separates from the church
> because of episcopal dispute . . . On the other hand, no schism
> fails to fabricate some heresy for itself, so that it might seem prop-
> erly to have withdrawn from the church.[24]

Not only ought one remain in unity with the bishops, but especially with the
See of Rome. When Meletius, Vitalis and Paulinus were in dispute about succession in Antioch, he wrote to Rome:

> I, following no leader but Christ, associate in communion with
> Your Beatitude [Damasus], that is, with the chair of Peter. I know
> that the church was founded upon that rock. Anyone at all who
> shall have eaten the Lamb outside of this house is impious. If one
> was not in the ark of Noah, he would have perished while the
> deluge held sway . . . I do not know Vitalis, I spit out Meletius, I
> do not know Paulinus. He who does not gather with you scatters.[25]

One of the contemporaries of Jerome was Saint Augustine, a man whose
enormous influence on succeeding ages can hardly be overstated. Born at Tagaste
in Numidia (in North Africa) in 354, he spent his earlier years in the acquisition

53

of knowledge and far removed from the active life of the Church. His story is too well known to need recounting here. It was not until 386 that his conversion was completed, and ten years later he was bishop of Hippo. His writing was, to a large extent, influenced by the forces around him—the heresies against which he fought. The Donatists, with their internal and spiritualized church (a doctrine they supplemented with a group of club-wielding enforcers known as Circumcellions) forced him to look at the presence in the Church of both good and bad, saints and sinners. He considered the efficacy of the sacraments as actions of the whole Church and not merely as actions of the minister. His dispute with Arianism (which is not as extensive as it was in the writings of the earlier Fathers) led him to examine the divinity of Christ. The doctrine of the Pelagians drew forth his theology of grace, free will, original sin and the necessity of the Church and sacraments for salvation. His own original adherence to the Manichaeans caused him to look at the humanity of Christ, the unified plan of the Old and New Testaments and the pre-existence of the Church. To attempt even to outline his theology would be a task far beyond our present scope. Instead, I will try simply to look at some of what he says about the Church.

Christ is mediator between God and man because Christ is both divine and human. This union of the divine and the human is paralleled by the union of Christ and his Church. This bond reveals to Augustine a sense of the Church as living, as a presence of Christ in the world. He writes:

> The whole Christ is the head and the body. The head, the only begotten Son of God, and the body of his church, bridegroom and bride, two in one flesh.[26]

> Therefore, let Christ speak, because in Christ the church speaks and in the church Christ speaks, and the body in the head and the head in the body.[27]

In the activity of the Spirit he sees the source of life for the body and, as others had also done, he compared the Spirit to the soul of that Body. The fact of this internal operation of the Spirit in the Church means that our lives as Christians are more than mere external conformity to a norm established by Christ. It is not simply as though Christ had set us an example or given us a law. Instead:

> The saints imitate Christ in order to follow after justice. But beyond this imitation his grace works our illumination and justification even from within . . . For this grace inserts into the body of Christ even baptized children, who are certainly not yet able to imitate anyone.[28]

There is a depth of awareness of true life in and through the Church. In the Church penance is preached and sin is forgiven, all in the name of Jesus. It is this living reality which has spread throughout the world. Augustine says:

> Nor do we say that we must believe we are in the church of Christ
> simply because Optatus of Milevis or Ambrose of Milan or the
> other innumerable bishops of our communion recommended that
> which we hold; nor because this church has preached in the coun-
> cils of our colleagues; nor because throughout the whole world in
> the holy places which our communion frequents so many wonders
> of unheard of things or cures have taken place . . . Whatever such
> things have taken place in the Catholic church, they are to be
> approved because they happened in the Catholic church; it is not
> therefore itself made known as catholic simply because these things
> have happened in it. The Lord Jesus himself, when he had risen
> from the dead and offered his body to be seen by the eyes of the
> disciples and touched by their hands (lest they think they were
> undergoing an illusion), judged that they ought to be strengthened
> even more by the testimony of the law and the prophets, showing
> those things now completed which so long before had been
> preached about him. Thus he also commended his church, saying
> that penance would be preached in his name and the remission of
> sins for the nations, by those who began from Jerusalem [Lk
> 24,4ff]. He bore witness that this was written in the law and the
> prophets and the psalms; we hold this to be recommended by his
> own mouth. These are the documents, these the foundations, these
> the groundwork of our cause.[29]

In the living Church the words of Jesus are fulfilled, and this is the sign of its
truthfulness. Like the other Fathers, Augustine points clearly and strongly to the
value of tradition and authority in the Church, an authority which resides in the
bishops and in the bishop of Rome particularly. Even the Scriptures have their
authority because they are the books of the Church, for who else could even
identify them? He says:

> If you find someone who does not yet believe in the gospel, what
> do you say to him when he says to you: "I do not believe"? Indeed,
> I would not believe in the gospel, were it not that the authority of
> the Catholic Church moves me.[30]

The authority of which he speaks is not simply a juridic sort of thing. It is far
more than that. Augustine expresses his awareness of this as he explains what it is
that keeps him in the Church. He says:

> In the Catholic Church (if I may omit the most sincere wisdom, to
> whose knowledge few spiritual men come in this life, so that they
> know it not because they are men, but still without doubt—not the

liveliness of understanding but the simplicity of belief keeps the rest of the crowd safe—if then I may omit this wisdom which you do not believe to be in the Catholic Church) there are many other things which quite rightly keep me in the bosom. The consent of peoples and nations holds me; an authority begun in miracles, nourished in hope, grown in charity, strengthened in age hold me; the succession of priests from the very See of Peter the apostle, into whose care the Lord commended his sheep after his resurrection, right down to the present episcopate holds me; finally the very name of "Catholic" holds me, for it is not without reason among so many heresies that this church alone has been so preserved that, although all the heresies would wish to be called catholic, still when some pilgrim asks where he may find the Catholic Church, none of the heretics dares to show him his own basilica or house.[31]

What he is really describing is what can be seen by the eyes of faith, that transposed understanding that we acquire in union with Christ. It is similar to the way in which he describes the faith of the Christian in the real presence of Christ in the Eucharist.

Jesus Christ willed to be known in the breaking of the bread by those whose eyes were held from recognizing him. The faithful know what I am saying; they recognize Christ in the breaking of the bread. Not all bread, but that which receives the blessing of Christ, is the body of Christ.[32]

It is my flesh, he says, for the life of the world [Jo 6,52]. The faithful know the body of Christ, if they do not overlook the body of Christ. They become the body of Christ if they will to live of the Spirit of Christ. Only the body of Christ lives from the Spirit of Christ . . . Whence comes [the statement] of Paul the Apostle when he explains his bread to us: As the bread, he says, so we the many are one body [I Cor 10,17]. O sacrament of piety! O sign of unity! O body of charity! He who wishes to live has a place to live and a source of life. Let him draw near, let him believe; let him be incorporated that he may be vivified.[33]

Nor need we merely look back at the past to see the reality of the signs of Christ's presence in the Church. For Augustine it is a living unity visible even now, just as it should be for us. The life of the Church is a sign that, with the eyes of faith, we should see and to which we should respond. Saint Paul so often called his converts to look into their own lives to see the presence of Christ. In a very powerful passage Augustine does the same:

Pay attention to me, the Church tells you; pay attention to me whom you see, even though you do not wish to see. Those who in those times were the faithful in the land of Judaea, being present learned as present all his divine words and deeds: the wonderful birth from a virgin, the passion, resurrection and ascension of Christ. You have not seen these things, for which reason you refuse to believe. Therefore, look to these things, gaze upon these, think of these things which you see, which are not narrated to you as past events, nor preached to you as future, but are pointed out as present. Or does it seem silly or unimportant to you, or do you think null and insignificant the divine miracle, that in the name of one who is crucified the whole race pursues its humanity.[34]

Augustine died at the age of 76 in the year 430, and when he died the world around him was in thorough upheaval. The constantly weakened empire had begun, finally, to come apart. He died in the third month of the siege of Hippo by the barbarian Vandals, and his death coincided with the end of the world as he had known it. But it was not the end of the Church as he had known it. By that time the centuries of reflection had given the Church an awareness of itself as a living reality, the Body of Christ, a visible and vital community. In fact, to a large extent it would be the Church's awareness of itself as community that would enable Europe to pass through the Dark Ages and emerge revitalized. And the Church would live still.

There remains only one more author to whom I wish to refer. He died in the year 450 in Gaul, and his name was Vincent of Lerins. The Abbey of Lerins had become a most active theological center by this time, and Vincent was one of those who worked and wrote there. About 434 he wrote his *Commonitorium*, in which he intended to set down a series of rules to aid in the determination of truth in times of controversy within the Church. I refer to his work now, because of things I have said above. I have indicated a living and growing self-consciousness in the Church. I would like to point out now that what I spoke of is not simply something that I am manufacturing and then reading back into the events that I have tried to describe. In the work of Vincent we find contemporary evidence that this reflection was self-conscious and that there was already an understanding of what was involved in it. When Vincent states his purpose, he says:

> Often with great zeal and the utmost attention, I have sought from
> many men endowed with holiness and learning a way in which I
> might discern in some certain and general and regular way the
> truth of the Catholic faith as opposed to the falseness of heretical
> depravity. From almost all of them I have always received an an-
> swer of this sort: That whether I or any other might wish to detect
> the deceits of rising heresies and to avoid snares and persevere
> whole and entire in the whole faith, he ought to guard his faith in

two ways, with the help of God. First with the authority of divine law, and then with the tradition of the Catholic Church. Here, perhaps, one might ask: "Since the canon of the Scriptures is complete and more than sufficient enough for all things, what necessity is there that the authority of ecclesiastical understanding be added to it?" The reason is that, because of its depth, not all receive the Sacred Scripture with one and the same meaning, but different people interpret its statements in different ways . . . And so it is quite necessary, because of the great prolixity of possible error, that the line of apostolic and prophetic interpretation be directed according to the norm of ecclesiastical and Catholic meaning. Likewise within the Catholic Church itself special care must be taken that we hold that which has been believed everywhere, always and by everyone . . . For that is truly and properly Catholic, which the very force and meaning of the word declare, which includes almost everything universally. But precisely this will result, if we follow universality, antiquity and consensus. We will follow universality in this way, if we confess as the one true faith that which the whole Church confesses throughout the world; [we will follow] antiquity, if we do not depart in any way from these meanings which it is clear that our holy ancestors and fathers stated; and in like manner, [we will follow] consensus, if, in that very antiquity, we keep following the definitions and opinions of all (or at least almost all) of the priests and teachers alike.[35]

These norms seem to relate clearly to the preservation of the teaching of the Church and its faith. What I spoke of, however, was more than that. It was not merely a matter of repeating the truth, but also of learning it. The life of the Church involved a self-reflection which opened it to an ever new self-awareness. To this also Vincent addresses himself:

But perhaps someone will say: "Will there be then no progress of religion in the Church of Christ?" Certainly there is, and the greatest [progress]. For who is so hostile to men, so hateful toward God, that he will try to prohibit it? Yet still in such a way that it is truly the progress of faith and not its transformation. It is a property of progress that each thing grow up to be itself; it is a property of change that something be changed from one thing to another. Therefore, the intelligence, the knowledge, the wisdom of one and all, of each man and of the whole Church, through the ages and centuries ought to grow and make great and vigorous progress, but only in its own kind, that is, in the same dogma, the same sense, the same meaning. Let the religion of souls imitate the pattern of bodies, which, although in the process of years they evolve and

unfold their numbers, still continue to be the same as they were . . .
For example: Our ancestors in times past sowed in the field of the
Church the seeds of wheaten faith; it is quite wicked and unsuit-
able that we, their offspring, should gather the false error of the
thistle in place of the genuine truth of the grain.[36]

In the beginning of this chapter I spoke of my realization that I did not have
to reinvent the wheel in order to discuss the Church as living community. I might
make use of that same analogy in another way. It is not necessary to reinvent the
wheel in order to achieve real theological progress. In fact, it would be totally
undesirable to do so. The Church is a living community, with a life that reaches
back to the death and resurrection of Jesus. It is not a community that begins
anew in each age. It is not a community devoid of a sense of its own history. And
its history is far more than the recounting of past events. It is a history that is far
more comparable to the personal history of an individual. Even as the individual
grows, he is still the same individual. The realities of his life in the present are
affected by those in the past, and he can never have an authentic grasp of his own
meaning if he does not realize this. So, too, the Church cannot be what it is and
what it is meant to be unless what it is now is the organic outgrowth of what it has
been. This is the truth. But it is a truth that can only be grasped by the mind and
heart transposed in the life of Christ. The point of view is, once more, absolutely
essential.

Notes

[1]Sister M. Melchoir Beyenka, OP, *The Father of the Church*. N.Y., 1954; H. von Campenhausen, *Ecclesiastical Authority and Spiritual Power in the Church of the First Three Centuries*. Stanford, 1969; F. Cayre, *Manual of Patrology and History of Theology*. 2 volumes, Paris, 1935; Varii, *Conciliorum ecumenicorum decreta*. Rome, 1962; *Corpus Scriptorum Ecclesiasticorum Latinorum editum consilio et impensis Academiae Litterarum Caesareae Vindebonensis* [CSEL]; H. Jedin, *Ecumenical Councils of the Catholic Church*. N.Y. 1960; W.A. Jurgens, *The Faith of the Early Fathers*. Collegeville, 1970; K.S. Latourette, *A History of Christianity*. N.Y., 1953; J.P. Migne, *Patrologiae cursus completus*. Series prima latine, Paris, 1844ff. [ML]; H.A. Musurillo, *The Fathers of the Primitive Church*. N.Y., 1966; R. Payne, *The Holy Fire*. N.Y., 1980; J. Quasten, *Patrology*. 3 volumes, Westminster, 1960-1962; M.J. Rouet de Journel, *Enchiridion patristicum loci SS. patrum, doctorum scriptorum ecclesiasticorum quos in usum Scholarum collegit*. Rome, 1959 [RJ]; R. Williams, *Christian Spirituality*. Atlanta, 1979; J.R. Willis, *The Teachings of the Church Fathers*. N.Y., 1966; D.W. Wuerl, *Fathers of the Church*. Boston, 1982.

[2]Ignatius, *Ep. ad Trall.* 9,1-2: Jurgens *op.cit.*, p. 21.

[3]Ignatius, *Ep. ad Rom.* 4,1: Jurgens, *op.cit.*, pp. 21-22.

[4]Ignatius, *Ep. ad Phila.* 7,1-2: Jurgens, *op cit.*, p. 23.

[5]Ignatius, *Ep. ad Phila.* 8,2: Jurgens, *op.cit.*, p. 23.

[6]Ignatius, *Ep. ad Smyrn.* 9,1-2: RJ 65.

[7]Irenaeus, *Adversus haereses* 3,3,1: RJ 209.

[8]*Ibid.* 4,26,2: RJ 237.

[9]*Ibid.* 3,3,2: RJ 210. The last sentence of the text reads as follows in Latin: Ad hanc enim ecclesiam, propter po[ten]tiorem principalitatem, necesse est omnem convenire ecclesiam, hoc est, eos qui sunt undique fideles, in qua semper ab his, qui sunt undique [vel: qui praesunt ecclesiis] conservata est ea quae est ab apostolis traditio. The Greek original has been lost.

[10]Cf. Clemens Romanus, *Ep. ad Cor.* 40,5; 42,2-4; 44,1-3; 57,1: RJ 19-20, 21, 27.

[11]Eusebius, *Hist. eccl.* 6,39,5: Quoted by Quasten, *op.cit.*, Vol. II, p. 40.

[12]Origen, *De principiis*. praef. 2: Quoted from Quasten, *op.cit.*, Vol. II, p. 59.

[13]*Ibid.*, praef. 3: RJ 444.

[14]Origen, *Contra Celsum*. 6,48: Quoted from Quasten, *op.cit.*. Vol. II, p. 82.

[15]Origen, *In Jesu Nave hom.*. Hom. 3, n.5: RJ 537.

[16]Cyprian, *Epist.* 55,8 (ad Antonianum): RJ 575.

[17]Cyprian, *Epist.* 59,14 (ad Cornelium): RJ 580.

[18]Cyprian, *De unitate ecclesiae.* 4,5: All of these passages are quoted from the translation by H.A. Musurillo, *op.cit.*. pp. 223-224; cf. RJ 555-556.

[19]CSEL, 3,2,744-745.

[20]Cyril of Jerusalem, *Catecheses* 18,23: RJ 838.

[21]*Ibid.* 18,26: RJ 839.

[22]Basil, *De Spiritu sancto* 27,66: RJ 954.

[23]Gregory of Nyssa, *Contra Eunomium* 4: RJ 1043.

[24]Jerome, *In epist. ad Tit.* 3,10: ML 598.

[25]Jerome, *Epist.* 15,2 (ad Damasum): ML 22,355; cf. RJ 1346.

[26]Augustine, *De unitate ecclesiae* 4,7: ML 43,395.

[27]Augustine, *Enar. in Ps 30* 1,4: ML 36,232.

[28]Augustine, *De peccatorum meritis et remissione* 1,9,10: RJ 1715.

[30]Augustine, *Contra epist. Manichaei quam vocant fundamenti* 5,6: RJ 1581.

[31]*Ibid.* 4,5: RJ 1580.

[32]Augustine, *Sermo* 234,2: RJ 1520.

[33]Augustine, *In Joannis evangelium tractatus* 26,13: RJ 1824.

[34]Augustine, *De fide rerum quae non vidientur* 4,7: RJ 1614.

[35]Vincent of Lerins, *Commonitorium* 2: RJ 2168.

[36]*Ibid.* 23: RJ 2174.

Chapter 4

A New Vision

It is now more than twenty years since I went to Mexico for a few months with another priest and a group of seminarians to work with the Maryknoll Fathers. We spent most of our time in Yucatan and were assigned to a variety of parishes. I was first in the village of Huhi and was then transferred to the island Cozumel. I have many fond memories of those days, and among them is the recollection of the beauty of both the island and the surrounding waters of the Gulf of Mexico. Part of my experience of those waters was more than recreational. On a number of days the sacristan and I would take a small boat and go out to catch fish for dinner. Most of the time I would row the boat and he would dive with a spear gun until he had two fish. There were a few times when I joined him in the water, but if our meals had depended on my success I would not now be writing this book—I would long since have died of starvation.

The point I want to make is not really about the fishing, but about the water. If you have never been in clear, tropical water it is hard even to imagine what it is like. You swim in a beauty that is startling. The sunlight reaches down hundreds of feet, filtered into a deeper and deeper blue. You are surrounded by a petrified forest of coral reef, inhabited by a living rainbow of tropical fish. It is like entering another world, where you are the stranger on display and the real inhabitants look at you and then go about their business. It is their world and you are merely a visitor. Yet it is a part of our world, too, even if we can only spend a limited time in it. The beauty of the sea is real, but it is just one facet of our experience of the full beauty of the world. For the fish it is the only experience of it.

What if it were possible for the fish to appreciate beauty as we can? And what then if we were to offer him the chance to come out of the water and see the rest of the world? If we could make such an offer, it would have to include a condition that might be less than desirable to this intelligent fish. That would be the condition of change. The fish would have to be transformed in some way so that he could live in the outside world. And suppose that such a change were possible but painful? Would he be willing to do it? We could tell him about what he would get to see and enjoy, but he would have to take our word for it until after the change had been completed. We could tell him that he would still enjoy the present beauty, albeit it in a new way, but there would be something further added. Could he, in faith, accept this, undergo the pain of his re-creation and then finally emerge into a new life? Or would he decide that what he already had was enough? He could then live and die where he already was, never knowing what he had missed.

We have heard the call of Christ to new life. We have considered the depth of the necessary transformation as we listened to Saint Paul describe an entrance into the life of God himself. We have seen the Fathers face martyrdom to achieve that goal. We have seen them cope with their limitations as they chose to obey the presence of Christ in the world in His Church. We have seen their gradually growing awareness of the implications of living in that Body of Christ, until they had arrived finally at an appreciation of hierarchical structure as well. And, as we were seeing their growth, we were looking at our own as well, for their history is our history. The life of the Church which they lived and described is the life of *our* Church. Jesus' proclamation of new life in the Kingdom was, at the same time, a proclamation of the need for transformation, no matter how painful that transformation might seem to be. Their experience, and ours as well, is not simply a losing of what we have in favor of something else. It is, instead, the pain of transposition, in which, while still being what we are, we also become something new. Our limited life is drawn into the limitless love of God. We yield our narrow vision so as to be able to see with his eyes, and as yet we do so in faith. We let go of our autonomy in order to obey his call, and in that obedience we are set free.

In a day when we hear so much of *dissent,* the real question for all of us should be one of *assent.* If we are, in fact, being drawn into a life so far beyond our present limits, then we should truly expect that such an assent will have aspects that to us will seem to have a certain degree of "blindness." This is part and parcel of faith. The Corinthians were called upon to live a new life, not because they had a philosophical explanation of its necessity, but because they were called to it by relationship to a crucified and risen Christ. The proof of it was not to be found in argumentation but in experience. The reality of the happiness to which they were being summoned could only be experienced as one yielded to it. The Fathers struggled to live that same life and in its living they began to see more clearly; but whatever clarity they achieved was always accompanied by the need to yield to the experience of a living Church, in the midst of which they experienced Christ himself. That call is ours as well.

Earlier I mentioned George MacDonald. In another of his sermons he speaks of the rich young man who came to Jesus and asked what he must do to gain eternal life. MacDonald's insights are magnificent. He speaks of the fact that the young man is really asking the wrong question. He is asking what he should *do* when the real question is one of *being* and not simply of doing. He was, in a sense, asking to possess the thing that should really possess him. MacDonald says:

> The Lord cared neither for isolated truth, nor for orphaned deed. It was truth in the inward parts, it was the good heart, the mother of good deeds, He cherished. It was the live, active knowing, breathing good He came to further. He cared for no speculation in morals or religion. It was good men He cared about, not notions of good things, or even good actions, save as the outcome of life, save as the bodies in which the primary live actions of love and will in the soul took shape and came forth. Could He by one word have set at rest all the questionings of philosophy as to the supreme good and the absolute truth, I venture to say that word He would not have uttered. But He would die to make men good and true. His whole heart would respond to the cry of sad publican or despairing pharisee, "How am I to be good?" . . .

> We have to do with Him to whom no one can look without the need of being good waking up in his heart; to think about Him is to begin to be good. To do a good thing is to do a good thing; to know God is to be good. It is not to make us do all things right He cares, but to make us hunger and thirst after a righteousness possessing which we shall never need to think of what is or is not good, but shall refuse the evil and choose the good by a motion of the will which is at once necessity and choice.[1]

We make a tremendous mistake when we think of morality in terms of simply weighing our actions by the measure of our own knowledge and that alone. Instead, we must grasp the fact that the living of a moral life is the experience of what we are in relationship to God and neighbor. We must see it in the context of our entrance into the life of the Trinity. We must see it as that hunger and thirst for righteousness which is a gift from God. And I mean not only that the righteousness is the gift, but that the hunger and thirst are gifts as well. Even the most cooling draught of clear, fresh water would not satisfy us if we had never experienced thirst. Both are gifts. This is why I would say that our first concern is not and should not be the weighing of actions in order to see the limits to which we can go. It should be the full and complete assent which opens us to the new life. Only then, as we begin to live that new life, can we truly make choices about our actions. The first reality is assent and not dissent. That assent involves a commitment to Christ, not in the abstract, but to Christ even as we experience him here and now—and that means as we experience him in and through the Church.

Our assent in faith is an assent to truth and an assent to a particular way of life which follows from that truth. The assent to truth may not seem so terribly difficult. So long as we focus on it simply as "truth" it will always seem just a bit abstract and assent to an abstraction is not overly onerous. But assent does not stop there. Assent to truth, if it be real assent, soon demands assent to a mode of life, assent to acting or not acting in certain ways. In this comes not only the idea of obedience to God, but the lived experience of that obedience. The proclamation of the truth makes demands upon us. No matter how good-willed we may be, we also experience our own sinfulness, and so there remains the temptation not to live the good. We experience our living of it as struggle, a struggle in which God's transforming grace seems at times painful to us. This is the experience of original sin.

It should be no surprise, then, that there will be discussions and disputes about doctrinal matters. This we should expect to emerge from the fact that what we believe cannot be captured by and limited to our human concepts. Nor should it come as a surprise that there will be discussions and disputes about moral matters. These may come from honest disagreement among believers. But we should be totally honest with ourselves and admit also that they may come from our unwillingness to confront our own sinfulness. Our dissent may arise from what we feel as the onus of that which is demanded of us by the truth.

In our own time we so often see the Church proclaiming something in the moral order, only to have that proclamation challenged by a society that does not want to hear demands. The same sort of challenge can even emerge from a desire to be kind to people, and to accept what they are doing because they seem to have so much trouble changing their way of life. But this attitude would not really be kind at all, since it would encourage people to continue living in a way that in the end can bring them nothing but harm. We all have the need to be confronted. Nor should it surprise us that so much of the dissent should come in the area of sexual morality. This is not because the Church in its moral teaching has a preoccupation with sex nor it is because sexual morality is the most important part of life, but because people can become so preoccupied with it. The Church must, therefore, address it. It is simply one of those areas affected by our original sinfulness and, like all areas so affected, it can become for us a source of struggle.

At the same time, the area of sexuality can serve us right now as a good example of what our Christian life demands in terms of assent. C.S. Lewis, in the book *Mere Christianity,* addresses this, and in the course of his presentation recognizes both the reality of a new vision and the struggle that we experience as we attempt to live it. Let me quote a part of what he says:

> Chastity is the most unpopular of the Christian virtues. There is no getting away from it: the old Christian rule is, "Either marriage, with complete faithfulness to your partner, or else total abstinence." Now this is so difficult and so contrary to our instincts, that obviously either Christianity is wrong or our sexual instinct, as it now is, has gone wrong. One or the other. Of course, being a Christian, I think it is the instinct which has gone wrong.
>
> But I have other reasons for thinking so. The biological purpose of sex is children, just as the biological purpose of eating is to repair the body. Now if we eat whenever we feel inclined and just as much as we want, it is quite true that most of us will eat too much: but not terrifically too much. One man may eat enough for two, but he does not eat enough for ten. The appetite goes a little beyond its biological purpose, but not enormously. But if a healthy young man indulged his sexual appetite whenever he felt inclined, and if each act produced a baby, then in ten years he might easily populate a small village. This appetite is in ludicrous and preposterous excess of its function.
>
> Or take it another way. You can get a large audience together for a strip-tease act—that is, to watch a girl undress on the stage. Now suppose you came to a country where you could fill a theatre by simply bringing a covered plate on to the stage and then slowly lifting the cover so as to let every one see, just before the lights went out, that it contained a mutton chop or a bit of bacon, would you not think that in that country something had gone wrong with the appetite for food? And would not anyone who had grown up in a different world think there was something equally queer about the state of the sex instinct among us?

Recall what I said in the first chapter about transposition in the ingestion of nutrients. There the act of eating, which we share in common with all living beings, was in us taken to the unimaginable level of entering into union with Christ in the Eucharist. What if we were to do the same thing with the concept of reproduction? The simple one-celled organism reproduces itself by dividing. The reproductive process becomes more and more complex as you ascend the biological ladder. In animals we see not just the reproductive fact, but an instinct which has reached a level of sensation and pleasure. In the human being it is this and still more. Here it involves a conscious choice, an interpersonal bond, a commitment in love. Then we have the added level of sacramentality. What is merely reproductive at the lowest level, is now consciously procreative in a Christian sense. The partners are procreative not only of the offspring of their sexual activity, but also of each other. This procreation has passed beyond the bounds of the simply biological and has entered into the realm of Christian procreation—the procreation of each other into a life of union with God and the procreation of children as children of God. What the Church calls us to in terms of the virtue of chastity is not merely a question of abstinence, but a positive reality. Our first experience of this may seem to be merely the acceptance of a prohibition of certain acts. In fact, what is really being offered to us is the opportunity to open ourselves to a new and fuller life. The Church calls us to see the real meaning of sex and to live in a new way. There is a transposition, in which the full meaning of the lower level can only be understood in terms of the higher.

This is but one example of the many areas in which we could acquire a deeper appreciation of what the Church is and does. I have already spoken of it in terms of its reality in the world as the living Body of Christ. As such it has the function, in its living and in its teaching, to proclaim the truth and to call all mankind to live that truth. It is a call to *be* what God means us to be, and it is only in so being that we can attain final happiness. What the Church *says* should emerge from what the Church *is*. There is in this a certain imperative of being. By this I mean that the teaching of the Church arises from what it, in fact, is in its union with Christ. If it is a means of salvation, then it should be capable of expressing that salvation and those things that are involved in its attainment. This should also imply that there will be a certain connatural level of reality that only gradually rises to the level of conceptualization. By this I mean that as the Church lives in union with Christ it becomes progressively more capable of putting that union into thought and words. It should not be unexpected, then, that there will be times in which the Church's "sense" of what is right may well precede its capacity to offer totally clear explanation as to why it is right. The "sense" is quite liable to emerge in the form of proclamation, while the conceptualized result emerges in a more extended doctrinal or practical teaching. Furthermore, there may be instances in which a moral norm is a matter of faith, demanding a commitment of obedience even when the "proof" of that norm cannot be reduced to purely rational argument. If the Church is truly Christ's Church, then both its proclamation and its teaching must be authentically his. The implication is, then, that there will be both development and authenticity, and these are topics that we will examine in succeeding chapters.

Both in ourselves and in the whole Church there is the reality of a new vision, leading us to new insight and new choices. To live in accord with this vision is also to experience the pain of going beyond ourselves. We live at times in the state of the fish who wants to emerge from the water—growing so that we can come forth in new life, but not yet there. But it is faith which allows us to be drawn onward, and the time will come when that faith can be set aside and we shall see face to face. When that happens we will finally know that what we experienced here as struggle was just our first taste of the fullest and most real freedom. Here we live with the thirst. There it will be satisfied.

Notes

[1] MacDonald, *op.cit.*, pp. 110–111.
[2] C.S. Lewis, *Mere Christianity*, Macmillan, N.Y., 1943, 1966, pp. 89–90.

Chapter 5

The Vision Grows

The little child takes his first step, and that tiny achievement is greeted with pride and wonder by the overjoyed parents. He takes a few more, and soon he can move from one piece of furniture to another as he sets out on a whole new era of exploration—an exploration which makes his parents pause to reconsider their former joy. There is almost always some minor disaster, after which everything breakable is moved to higher shelves. He tiptoes around, in a form of locomotion frequently interrupted by sudden seatings—answering the question of why babies need such soft bottoms. Unscathed he goes on his way, fortunate that his own smallness makes his fall so short. He grows and his steps become sure. He goes where he wills. Even as an adult he will sometimes stumble or fall, but he has learned to walk. The halting step was the first sign of the development that would eventually lead to maturity.

The concept of a necessary and legitimate development in the teaching of the Church had appeared in the writings of Vincent of Lerins, but for a long time in the history of theology that notion of development was not itself further developed. Then, in the last century, one of the Church's greatest writers set himself the task of its examination. Cardinal Newman, in the process of his own conversion, studied the question and produced *An Essay on the Development of Christian Doctrine*—an "essay" of more than four hundred pages, looking not only at theory but at a multiplicity of practical examples. I will touch upon some of the relevant themes that he develops, and I would suggest that the reader pursue these thoughts by reading what Newman himself has to say.

His approach is above all one of common sense. If we truly believe that God has revealed Himself in this world, then what would that revelation entail? Could we expect, even before we set out to examine it, that there would be some sort of progressive development? Could we expect that there would be given to us in this life some infallible organ of communicating that revelation? As to the progressive character of revelation, Newman sees immediately that there is development to be expected. He writes:

> If Christianity is a fact, and impresses an idea of itself on our minds and is a subject-matter of exercises of the reason, that idea will in course of time expand into a multitude of ideas, and aspects of ideas, connected and harmonious with one another, and in themselves determinate and immutable, as is the objective fact itself which is thus represented. It is a characteristic of our minds, that they cannot take an object in, which is submitted to them simply and integrally. We conceive by means of definition or description; whole objects do not create in the intellect whole ideas, but are, to use a mathematical phrase, thrown into series, into a number of statements, strengthening, interpreting, correcting each other, and with more or less exactness approximating, as they accumulate, to a perfect image . . .

> And the more claim an idea has to be considered living, the more various will be its aspects; and the more social and political is its nature, the more complicated and subtle will be its issues, and the longer and more eventful will be its course. And in the number of these special ideas, which from their very depth and richness cannot be fully understood at once, but are more and more clearly expressed and taught the longer they last,—having aspects many and bearings many, mutually connected and growing one out of another, and all parts of a whole, with a sympathy and correspondence keeping pace with the ever-changing necessities of the world, multiform, prolific and ever resourceful,—among these great doctrines surely we Christians shall not refuse a foremost place to Christianity. Such previously to the determination of the fact, must be our anticipation concerning it from a contemplation of its initial achievements.[1]

For some this comes as a surprise; even, perhaps, a bit of a shock. The doctrine of the Church must develop? How can that be? Here we are dealing with an action of God. Would not the communication of that revelation be perfect, just as God intended it, and so not subject to progress? Newman responds that, even in the case of revelation, such progress is to be expected. Perhaps, even, especially in the case of revelation, since here we are concerned with the limited minds of men attempting to grasp the unlimited reality of God. In other words, to speak of the need for development is not at all to lessen the perfection of God. It is simply to accept the limitations of the human recipient. He says:

> It may be objected that its inspired documents at once determine the limits of its mission without further trouble; but ideas are in the writer and reader of the revelation, not the inspired text itself: and the question is whether those ideas which the letter conveys from writer to reader, reach the reader at once in their completeness and accuracy on his first perception of them, or whether they open out in his intellect and grow to perfection in the course of time . . .

> Nor can it fairly be made a difficulty that thus to treat of Christianity is to level it in some sort to sects and doctrines of the world, and to impute to it the imperfections which characterize the productions of man. Certainly it is a sort of degradation of a divine work to consider it under an earthly form; but it is no irreverence, since our Lord Himself, its Author and Guardian, bore one also. Christianity differs from other religions and philosophies, in what is superadded to earth from heaven; not in kind, but origin; not in its nature, but in its personal characteristics; being informed and quickened by what is more that intellect, by a divine spirit. It is externally what the Apostle calls an "earthen vessel," being the religion of men. And, considered as such, it grows "in wisdom and stature;" but the powers which it wields, and the words which proceed out of its mouth, attest its miraculous nativity.[2]

Within the Scriptures, Newman sees that there is more than a simple accumulation of disparate facts one after another. What is communicated to man is his relationship to God, not merely facts about it. In a sense, then, the whole truth is communicated in each age, but man's grasp is always partial and incomplete. He says:

> It is not that first one truth is told, then another; but the whole truth or large portions of it are told at once, yet only in their rudiments, or in miniature, and they are expanded and finished in their parts, as the course of revelation proceeds.[3]

From this fact of development, however, there also emerges a considerable problem. If developments occur, then we must have some means of ascertaining in

70

what way they are true. We must be able to differentiate between the authentic development and those trends that move in wrong directions. This is no easy task, because we live within the very process of development we are attempting to examine and our own limitations can easily confuse one with the other. It is one thing to realize that there will be development and quite another to have full clarity about what such development will contain. Again he writes:

> It has now been made probably that developments of Christianity were but natural, as time went on, and were to be expected; and that these natural and true developments, as being natural and true, were of course contemplated and taken into account by its Author, who in designing the work designed its legitimate results. These, whatever they turn out to be, may be called absolutely "the developments" of Christianity. That, beyond reasonable doubt, there are such is surely a great step gained in the inquiry; it is a momentous fact. The next question is, *What* are they? and to a theologian, who could take a general view, and also possessed an intimate and minute knowledge, of its history, they would doubtless on the whole be easily distinguishable by their own characters, and require no foreign aid to point them out, no external authority to ratify them. But it is difficult to say who is exactly in this position. Considering that Christians, from the nature of the case, live under the bias of the doctrines, and in the very midst of the facts, and during the process of the controversies, which are to be the subject of criticism, since they are exposed to the prejudices of birth, education, place, personal attachment, engagements, and party, it can hardly be maintained that in matter of fact a true development carries with it always its own certainty even to the learned, or that history, past or present, is secure from the possibility of a variety of interpretations.[4]

Newman envisions the possibility of intellectual testing of the validity of developments, but he discounts these as not being finally decisive. The reason is that the tests would be themselves part of the controversy that might be in progress. They would be efforts at explanation within the framework of the science of theology; but they could lack the practical capacity to render final decisions and insure the accuracy of that decision. They would be instruments of decision rather than guarantees of the value of the decision. Therefore, the means of determining the legitimacy of development must be in some way external to the development itself.[5]

Ultimately he comes to the conclusion that the guarantor of the validity of development, the visible teacher in this world, must be found in the Church. It is the Magisterium (the teaching authority) of the Church which can guarantee its truth. This is not because those who exercise this teaching function are the most learned and can therefore give the most convincing reasons. It is, rather, because God's communication of revelation, and the consequent and necessary development implied by that revelation, demand it. Revelation demands authority. Otherwise, how is it ever to be recognized and accepted? the very fact that it is *revelation* means that it is not the simple product of human intelligence, even though intelligence can be brought to bear upon it and can begin to grasp its implications. But in the final analysis, it is the revelation itself which verifies the truth of its content and not human reason in itself. At the heart of this is clearly what I had spoken of earlier—a new vision. There is a totally new point of view involved in our acceptance of revelation, and the effort to attempt to subject everything once again to reason alone would mean the loss of that vision. It would be the effort to explain the transposed from an untransposed point of view, and as such it would be doomed to failure.

There is a clear need for what the Church has, in fact, always seen itself as having—a charism to teach authentically and, indeed, infallibly if need be. This is precisely what we saw in the earliest of the Church's writers. It was there still in process of discovery. Note carefully, I say discovery and not invention. It was not something made up by those in the Church. It was a gift given to the Church and the process of life led to the realization of what it meant. It would remind one of the child's growing awareness of the implications of his own ability to grasp the meaning of reality. It is an ability that he uses even before he can explain what it is. As he grows and learns still more, he can begin to reflect on and put into words what his intelligence means. But it is a reality even before he says so.

There is, in the life of the Church, a confirmation of all that has been said. Common sense itself demands that there be a completely trustworthy authority which can point out to us the truth of what we say in regard to the revelation. Such authority does *not* mean that there will be in the world some person or persons who have immediate access to all the answers of all the questions that can arise. It does *not* mean that there must be a person or group of persons who can never make a mistake in any way at all. But it *does mean* that there should be some person or persons visibly in a position to guide and direct the members of the Church to the truth. Such a person or persons should also be able to guide the course of the Church's life, especially in moments of serious crisis and serious indecision, when theologians are in dispute and it is evident that their learning and intelligence are, in fact, not supplying the solution to the problems which confront members of the Church in living Christian life. What is demanded is not further argumentation, but the gift of a practical wisdom which can direct the events of life along the right course, even when the explanation of such events is still in process of development. This wisdom can be seen in the way in which the charism of teaching is exercised in the hierarchical structure of the Church. If assurance of truth depended ultimately only on the rational argumentations of those in dispute, then no member of the Church could be sure of real contact with the revelation of God until he had first of all based his acceptance in the process of his own intellectual assessment of the arguments. Yet, what is actually needed is a totally trustworthy guide for the concrete living of life. I said that this is confirmed in the life of the Church. What I mean is that, on the one hand, such an authority seems absolutely necessary and, on the other, it does not seem to appear anywhere in the world except in the Church. Once again, let us listen to Newman:

> The common sense of mankind does not support a conclusion thus forced upon us by analogical considerations. It feels that the very idea of revelation implies a present informant and guide, and that an infallible one; not a mere abstract declaration of Truths unknown before to man, or a record of history, or the result of an antiquarian research, but a message and lesson speaking to this man and that. This is shown by the popular notion which has prevailed among us since the Reformation, that the Bible itself is such a guide; and which succeeded in overthrowing the supremacy of Church and Pope, for the very reason that it was a rival authority, not resisting merely, but supplanting it. In proportion, then, as we find, in matter of fact, that the inspired Volume is not adapted or intended to subserve that purpose, are we forced to revert to that living and present Guide, who, at the era of our rejection of her, had been so long recognized as the dispenser of Scripture, according to times and circumstances, and the arbiter of all true doctrine and holy practice to her children. We feel a need, and she alone of all things under heaven supplies it. We are told that God has spoken. Where? In a book? We have tried it and it disappoints; it disappoints us, that most holy and blessed gift, not from fault of its own, but because it is used for a purpose for which it was not given. The Ethiopian's reply, when St. Philip asked him if he understood what he was reading, is the voice of nature: "How can I, unless some man shall guide me?" The Church undertakes that office; she does what none else can do, and this is the secret of her power. "The human mind," it has been said, "wishes to be rid of doubt in religion; and a teacher who claims infallibility is readily believed on his simple word. We see this constantly exemplified in the case of individual pretenders among ourselves. In Romanism the Church pretends to it; she rids herself of competitors by forestalling them. And probably, in the eyes of her children, this is not the least persuasive argument for her infallibility, that she alone of all Churches dares claim it, as if a secret instinct and involuntary misgivings restrained those rival communions which go so far towards affecting it." These sentences, whatever be the errors of their wording, surely express a great truth. The most obvious answer, then, to the question, why we yield to the authority

of the Church in the questions and developments of faith, is, that some authority there must be if there is a revelation given, and other authority there is none but she. A revelation is not given, if there be no authority to decide what it is that is given.[6]

Does this presence of an infallible authority then imply that somehow theology is of no use? Does it mean that our intellectual activities are valueless and that we should simply wait for answers from authority? By no means. But it does clearly imply that theology and authority must work together to arrive at the truth. It means, as was implied some chapters earlier, that there is an organic relationship between the parts of the Body.

In other words, theology can examine and learn and speculate. It can instruct. It can help the whole Church in the deepening of its awareness of life in Christ. The magisterial authority in the Church is also involved in this positive process. At the same time, the fact that it is authority will give it a function that may appear to be negative. It may point out the limits to speculation, even when theology as a science cannot prove the location of those limits by argument alone. It may also legitimately proclaim a truth which theology cannot "prove." In this instance theology would then be bound to take this truth into account in any further study. This also would place a limit for the theologian—perhaps not so much a boundary stone as a guidepost.

The depth of insight gained by the application of the intellect to revealed truth can lead us to greater depths of our awareness of union in Christ. The direction of that intellectual activity can be verified and, at times, forewarned by the function of authority. Newman says:

> Ignorance, misapprehension, unbelief, and other causes, do not at once cease to operate because the revelation is in itself true and in its proofs irrefragable. We have then no warrant at all for saying that an accredited revelation will exclude the existence of doubts and difficulties on the part of those whom it addresses, or dispense with anxious diligence on their part, though it may in its own nature tend to do so. Infallibility does not interfere with moral probation; the two notions are absolutely distinct. It is no objection then to the idea of a peremptory authority, such as I am supposing, that it lessens the task of personal inquiry, unless it be an objection to the authority of Revelation altogether. A Church, or a Council, or a Pope, or a Consent of Doctors, or a Consent of Christendom, limits the inquiries of the individual in no other way than Scripture limits them: it does limit them; but, while it limits their range, it preserves intact their probationary character; we are tried as really, though not on so large a field. To suppose that the doctrine of permanent authority in matters of faith interferes with our free-will and responsibility is, as before, to forget that there were infalli-

ble teachers in the first age, and heretics and schismatics in the ages subsequent . . . Moreover, those who maintain that Christian truth must be gained solely by personal efforts are bound to show that methods, ethical and intellectual, are granted to individuals sufficient for gaining it; else the mode of probation they advocate is less, not more, perfect than that which proceeds upon external authority.[7]

It is clear that the Church does not begin its existence as a group which has been given a set of doctrines and dogmas, ready-made and simply to be brought forth as occasion warrants. It is, rather, a living community, the Body of Christ. It has been brought into union with the life of God Himself and this unity has transformed its being. It has been given new eyes, with which it beholds a new vision. It sees reality, not simply with its old, human eyes, but with the eyes of faith. With those eyes it looks at the world, at itself, at the meaning of its own life. It begins to express itself and that expression continues for all the centuries of its existence. Just as we see and evaluate new things all the days of our lives, so too does the Church. Even in the newest of circumstances it brings its vision and its wisdom to bear. And every new reality must be judged in the light of what it has already learned—otherwise, what value would experience have? How could any of us learn anything new if we failed to bring it into the framework of what we already know? The truths the Church has already learned and expressed become the touchstone of its interpretation of what it now confronts. Its own lived experience enables it to interpret what it finds in this present day. This is what we speak of as tradition. It is the already learned experience of the living Body of Christ. In its light all that is new must be seen. To grasp and interpret and express this tradition must, of necessity, be one of the functions of those in authority in the Church.

The process of development of self-understanding in the Church involves all of its members. Not all of them, as individuals, are going to be in perfect step as this process continues. Some will seem to be taking that first faltering step, some will seem to be walking steadily and resolutely, some will be sitting surprised on their bottoms. But if any are to know with certainty that they are walking in the right direction, there must be someone with the ability to say so. Not someone who knows everything for every time, but someone who does indeed know how to look with the eyes of faith. Someone who is visibly in a position to teach and to decide. Someone who can take into account all that is being said and then say in return that this does indeed (or perhaps does not) accord with the already lived experience, the tradition, of this Body of Christ. That such persons should exist seems to be demanded by common sense; but there is also the need for faith. There is the need to believe that God cares enough about the Church and about His own truthfulness that He will, with His grace, protect those in leadership so that they can carry out this necessary function.

75

Finally, I think we should all remember that we are indeed in process. We are not yet complete. We need to be humble enough to realize that what we see as progress must *always* be weighed against the already existing tradition. At times we will find that what we were so sure of has been found wanting; at other times we will be delighted to see that our certainty was justified. But we must always remember that we never stop learning, and that our learning process is deceptive when it become separated from what the Church already teaches.

On the other hand, the fact that we falter should not be a source of discouragement. In the end, we are called to perfection. We have not yet attained it. George MacDonald, in speaking of the keeping of the commandments and our halting efforts to achieve their keeping, says something that seems appropriate here.

> That no keeping but a perfect one will *satisfy* God, I hold with all my heart and strength; but that there is none else He cares for, is one of the lies of the enemy. What father is not pleased with the first tottering attempt to his little one to walk? What father would be satisfied with anything but the manly step of the full-grown son?[8]

Notes

[1]John Henry Cardinal Newman, *An Essay on the Development of Christian Doctrine*, Christian Classics, Westminster, MD, 1845, 1878, 1968, pp. 55–56.

[2]*Ibid*, pp. 57–57.

[3]*Ibid*, p. 64.

[4]*Ibid*, pp. 75–76.

[5]*Ibid*, p. 78.

[6]*Ibid*, pp. 87–89.

[7]*Ibid*, pp. 82–83.

[8]George MacDonald, *op.cit.*, p. 113.

Chapter 6

Thou Shalt Not . . .

Earlier I used the example of the child learning to walk. From this I would like now to draw a further lesson. When you learned to walk, you did not do so by first having someone explain it to you and then, having found out the do's and don't's of walking, you grew legs and began to do it. The legs and feet were already there. Babies seem to have the idea, at first, that feet are to play with and nibble on. It would be a shame if it all stopped right there. The whole world would sit around biting its toes and no one would ever get anywhere. Instead, observation, experiment and practice soon led us to an awareness of what we could really do with those feet. We needed some help. Our parents held our hands and supported us and soon got us moving. We learned to run and jump and even, perhaps, to dance. The athlete or the dancer learns a lot of rules about what to do or not do in the use of those appendages. The fact of what legs are leads us to know how to use them.

Christian life involves the reality of what we are and the way in which we live as a result of what we are. Two things: What we are and how we live. The first is expressed in doctrine, the second in morality. Frequently enough we get the impression that the morality is the more essential. This is not really the case. What I mean by this is that the doctrine tells us of the fact of our relationship to God and of what we *are* as a result of that relationship. The doctrine of the Trinity is not simply a question of a theory about the inner life of the Divinity. If we see it, for example, within the framework of what we have learned from First Corinthians, then we begin to realize that what we believe about the Trinity is also revealing to us who and what we are. It reveals to us our relationship to God and our entrance into His life. From this follows a new way of living. It is really from doctrine that morality flows.

The morality, however, is essential. It is not as though we become Christian by following a certain set of rules. Rather, by virtue of the fact that, through the *gift* of God, we are Christian a certain mode of life follows. Not to live in that newness of life is a form of self-destruction, because our failure to do so does violence to ourselves. It cuts away at our integrity by separating our actions from the reality of our existence. In a sense, we might say that our actions are not the source of what we are so much as they are the visible signs or symptoms of what are or, at least, of what we are choosing to become.

Both doctrinal and moral teachings are necessary. However, we find often enough that the moral teaching is more of a problem to us. It is here that we feel the demands, and become acutely aware of what Paul was talking about in the Epistle to the Romans, when he spoke of finding himself doing the things he did not want to do and not doing the things he did want to do. For this reason, in the next few pages I am going to concentrate especially on the question of morality— not one particular norm, but morality in general.

When the Church deals with moral issues, what is it attempting to do? On the surface it speaks in terms of rules and laws: Do this; don't do that. In fact, a great deal of moral teaching assumes the form of prohibition. There is a very good reason for this. Positive teaching is essential, yet it doesn't always leave us in a state of clarity. When we tell someone, "Do good!" we are telling him a fine thing. But, what good shall he do? What if he has a choice of five or six good things that can be done, but doing one of them will make it impossible to do the others? He can come to the aid of any one of a number of people in need, but giving his time to one of them allows no time for the others. The commandment is real, but carrying it out takes further discernment. Negative norms, on the other hand, always seems to have greater precision. "Do not steal." This does not mean that you do not steal from this person or that, but that you do not steal from any person whatsoever. In a sense we might say that the positive norms point us in the direction of the proper use of our freedom, while the negative norms set the limits beyond which that freedom will be misused and abused.

There is, to be sure, within any community (including the Church) a certain amount of disciplinary regulation for the good order of the community. A portion of Canon Law would fall into this category. There are, for example, norms for the proper conduct of the Liturgy, and many of those norms regulate things that in themselves are arbitrary, but which are defined with a certain uniformity for the good of all. When we deal with real moral norms, however, we are dealing with more than simple legislation. One way to explain this is to look carefully at the *images* present in our own minds when we think of morality. Such images have a lot to do with how we view reality.

One image of morality is what I would call the legal image. Here morality is seen as a set of laws. There is, in the minds of many, a parallel with morality and civil or canonical law. We may find ourselves thinking of morality in terms of things like traffic laws. The traffic laws set a speed limit, which in most places is fifty-five miles per hour. Surely a speed of fifty-six would not be significantly more dangerous. Probably sixty is not much more of a peril. Then again, fifty would be just a bit safer. There is something arbitrary in the decision. Yet a decision has to be made, and once it is made then, technically, anyone who goes any amount over that speed is breaking law. The legislators chose a speed within a safe range and made that the norm. In its simplest form it is a prohibitive statement: "Do not drive over fifty-five." They could have chosen another speed, and they could change it in the future. The law is binding while it is in effect, but it is subject to change. This is the way in which some envision moral law as well.

How often have you read in the newspapers or heard on television such phrases as "the Catholic *ban* on birth control" or "the Catholic *ban* on abortion"? As though it were a question of no more than a rule imposed on Catholics, but a rule which authority could simply change if only it would choose to do so. This is what I mean by a legal image, and as long as that is our image of morality we will never really understand what morality is all about.

There is another kind of image which offers a better insight. This image still involves statements that sound like simple prohibitive rules, but they have a far deeper significance. For example, how many times have you seen a bottle with a label that read: "Do not use internally"? You can, of course, use it internally if you want to. If you do so, you may die. You could write to the company and get their permission to do it. Even if they granted the permission, you would still die. What we have here is more than legal prohibition. The statement is pointing to a deeper reality. The contents of this bottle and your life are incompatible. This is a much better picture of what is meant by moral law.

Real moral prohibitions point to realities which are incompatible with your life and which may cause death. There is no element of the arbitrary here. The person who told you that you had permission to use the product internally would be telling you to go ahead and die, and his permission could not change that result. This is why the Church's statements on morality are far more than a "ban." They are statements of fact. They are not just laws. A law, such as a traffic law, may carry a penalty with it; but that penalty is not imposed if the lawbreaker is not discovered. The law also is intended to insure safety, but even then the violator may get by without an accident. In either case, there is no detrimental effect. But in the case of the poison the "punishment" is contained right in the "violation." Drinking the poison causes death. The same is true of moral law. It is not as though the violator, if caught, will be punished. In fact, his action is self-destructive. The moral "law" attempts to point this out. The Church is not presenting a "ban" for Catholics. It is simply expressing a truth, and could *not,* even if it wanted to, give permission to break this "rule." To do so would be simply to lie.

It should be noted also that the real harm of the violation of moral norms is a harm that comes to the *violator* ultimately, even though he may not at first be aware of it. If you think through the implications of morality, this becomes evident. For example, we are told: "Thou shalt not steal." If I go ahead and steal anyway, then I take another person's property and cause him at least an inconvenience and, perhaps, even considerable harm. But I am hurting *myself* even more! I am, in effect, saying that the other person is of no value and has no rights, that my desires for his property outweigh his claim to what is his. In a sense, I have depersonalized him. Actually, I have not reduced his person, except in my own mind. But that reduction in my own mind is significant. I am implying that, if he has no rights and I can wilfully take what is his, then neither do I have any rights and someone stronger than I can come along and take what I have. I have begun to destroy myself by isolating myself from God and neighbor.

This sort of depersonalizing takes places in any sin, and in some areas it is even more harmful and seems to go deeper than it does in the preceding example. Anyone who lived through the last days of the Second World War can recall vividly the horror stories that emerged from the liberation of the death camps. Millions of Jews and others were slaughtered. They were treated as non-persons, and their lives meant nothing. This was a dreadful effect of sin. But there was, I would say, an even more catastrophic effect on the perpetrators of these atrocities. What did it do to them as persons? What was its internally destructive effect? Sin is like a stone thrown into still water, and its ripples spread out and cause pain in many others. But it is the one who caused the ripple who sinks.

Many of the harmful effects of sin follow even if the sinner is not really blameworthy for his actions. In that case, the external harm may be there, but the sinner, by reason of whatever removes his culpability, may avoid destroying himself. Moral teaching, however, must face both of these realities. It must call each of us to see the real meaning of our actions both internally and externally, so that this destructive force can be removed. This is what we are talking about when we speak of certain actions as intrinsically evil. It means that there are certain things which, even if we are not culpable in their performance, will cause harm nonetheless. And if we are culpable—if we know what we are doing and choose to do it—they will destroy us.

One other point is also deserving of some explanation. It is so easy for any of us to look at the Church's moral teaching and to realize that we are not acting in accord with it. We are then faced with the need either to change or to justify our position. We may feel as though the Church's attitude is judgmental and we can easily resent that. But that misses the truth of the matter. What the Church is

80

calling us to is a life in union with God, a life that will give us the fullest happiness and self-fulfillment. The Church, in its statements on morality, is saying, "Do not do this, because it will destroy you. It will undermine the fulfillment of all that you can ever hope for." The Church, if it is really to act in the name of God, *must* care about each of its members. In this attitude of the Church we are experiencing something of the love of God become incarnate in this world. C.S. Lewis, in *The Problem of Pain* speaks of the power of God's love—a love which calls us beyond ourselves. He says:

> By the goodness of God we mean nowadays almost exclusively His lovingness; and in this we may be right. And by Love, in this context, most of us mean kindness—the desire to see others than the self happy; not happy in this way or in that, but just happy. What would really satisfy us would be a God who said of anything we happened to like doing, "What does it matter so long as they are contented?" We want, in fact, not so much a Father in Heaven as a grandfather in heaven—a senile benevolence who, as they say, "liked to see young people enjoying themselves," and whose plan for the universe was simply that it might be truly said at the end of each day, "a good time was had by all." Not many people, I admit, would formulate a theology in precisely those terms: but a conception not very different lurks at the back of many minds. I do not claim to be an exception: I should very much like to live in a universe which was governed on such lines. But since it is abundantly clear that I don't, and since I have reason to believe, nevertheless, that God is Love, I conclude that my conception of love needs correction. I might, indeed, have learned, even from the poets, that Love is something more stern and splendid than mere kindness . . .
>
> A father half apologetic for having brought his son into the world, afraid to restrain him lest he should create inhibitions or even to instruct him lest he should interfere with his independence of mind, is a most misleading symbol of the Divine Fatherhood.[1]

The love of God in itself, and as expressed in the life of the Church, makes demands upon us, because that love is powerful and transformative. Love is not mere "kindness"—a false kindness, at that—which simply allows people to trudge along in a comfortable rut. It is more than we sometimes bargain for. Again Lewis says:

> When Christianity says that God loves man, it means that God *loves* man; not that He has some "disinterested," because really indifferent, concern for our welfare, but that, in awful and surprising truth, we are the objects of His love. You asked for a loving

81

God: you have one. The great spirit you so lightly invoked, the "lord of terrible aspect," is present: not a senile benevolence that drowsily wishes you to be happy in your own way, not the cold philanthropy of a conscientious magistrate, nor the care of a host who feels responsible for the comfort of his guests, but the consuming fire Himself, the Love that made the world, persistent as the artist's love for his work and despotic as a man's love for a dog, provident and venerable as a father's love for a child, jealous, inexorable, exacting as love between the sexes. How this should be, I do not know: it passes reason to explain why any creatures, not to say creatures such as we, should have a value so prodigious in their Creator's eyes. It is certainly a burden of glory not only beyond our deserts but also, except in rare moments of grace, beyond our desiring . . .[2]

We are called to happiness, to perfection, to completion. We are called to be all that we ever could desire to be. We are called to be one with Christ. To respond to this call means to submit ourselves in obedience to God. It also means submission in obedience to the Church, through which God makes himself present to us. Precisely what this obedience to the Church means we shall look at further on; but, for the moment, let us look first at the simple fact. Nowhere, except in God, will we find completion. For this reason we had better pay close attention to our tendency to rationalize, our tendency to avoid the self-confrontation that the love of God and the teaching of the Church bring about. To quote Lewis once more:

We are bidden to "put on Christ," to become like God. That is, whether we like it or not, God intends to give us what we need, not what we now think we want. Once more, we are embarrassed by the intolerable compliment, by too much love, not too little.

Yet perhaps even this view falls short of the truth. It is not simply that God has arbitrarily made us such that He is our only good. Rather God is the only good of all creatures: and by necessity, each must find its good in that kind and degree of the fruition of God which is proper to its nature. The kind and degree may vary with the creature's nature: but that there ever could be any other good, is an atheistic dream. George Macdonald, in a passage I cannot now find, represents God as saying to men, "You must be strong with my strength and blessed with my blessedness, *for I have no other to give you.*" That is the conclusion of the whole matter. God gives what He has, not what He has not: He gives the happiness that there is, not the happiness that is not. To be God—to be like God and to share His goodness in creaturely response—to be miserable—these are the only three alternatives. If we will not learn to eat the only food that the universe grows—the only good that any possible universe ever can grow—then we must starve eternally.[3]

The love of God, and that same love as it exists in the Church, is demanding. Not with the sort of demand that comes from a tyrant acting in an arbitrary way, but with the demand that comes from truth. To know the truth and then not to live in accord with it is a sure and certain way to tear ourselves apart internally. That is precisely what sin does.

Notes

[1]C.S. Lewis, *The Problem of Pain*, Macmillan, N.Y., 1940, 1962, pp. 39–40, 41.
[2]*Ibid*, pp. 46–47.
[3]*Ibid*, pp. 54–54.

Chapter 7

Man and Superman

Who in the world has been making up all these rules about morality? And can't we find him and tell him to stop it? Well, in a sense no one has been making them up. And, in another sense, everyone has. The source of morality is not some person or persons who had a bright idea and decided to draw up directions about it. The source is somewhere else entirely; this we can see, as we realize that we all find certain moral norms hard to accept for ourselves, although we may be ready enough to appeal to them when we are rubbed the wrong way by someone else. Why is that?

It's easy enough to see that when we apply the rules to someone else we are appealing to something that we think the other person should see as objective and not just as our private rules. But if the norms are objective, then why do we sometimes struggle against them in our own lives? They make demands. There is the reason. That is not comfortable if the demand runs counter to what we would prefer to do. Then why not simply throw out the rules we don't like? Why struggle at all? Yet we do struggle and we feel remorse when we act contrary to what we accept as right. It would seem that these moral norms must be far more than just the result of our own decisions. They seem to emerge from our minds and hearts in such a way that acting contrary to them does violence to us. We may find them hard to keep at times; yet, in some way, we find it even harder not to.

Jeremiah, the Old Testament prophet, was a hesitant spokesman for God. His call is recounted in the first chapter of the book which bears his name, and it is a call to which he responds—but with considerable reluctance.[1] "Ah, Lord God," he says, "I cannot speak; for I am only a youth." He is promptly told, "Do not say, 'I am only a youth;' for to all to whom I send you shall you go, and all that I command you shall speak." In his vision he sees God reach out to touch his mouth and there to place the word of God. So he goes about his preaching, and soon finds out that he doesn't like it one bit. What he must preach is not what people want to hear. Who really ever does want to hear corrections and admonitions and reprimands—unless, of course, they are directed at someone else? He is greeted, not with enthusiasm, but with indifference, rejection and even, finally, with plots against his life. Prophesying was not all it was cracked up to be!

Why did not Jeremiah simply stop preaching? He was certainly tempted to quit—this is quite clear in the book itself and is not just a matter of conjecture. He makes his complaint to God. This business of being a prophet had lost its glamour. The romance was gone. The honeymoon was over. He says:

Thou hast duped me, O Lord, and I let myself be duped;
Thou hast been too strong for me, and has prevailed.
I have become a laughing-stock all day long,
Everyone mocks me.
As often as I speak, I must cry out,
I must call, "Violence and spoil!"
For the word of the Lord has become to me
A reproach and derision all day long.
If I say, "I will not think of it,
Nor speak any more in his name,"
It is in my heart like a burning fire,
Shut up in my bones;
I am worn out with holding it in—
I cannot endure it.
For I hear the whispering of many,
Terror all around.
"Denounce him! let us denounce him!"
Say all my intimate friends, who watch for my tripping;
"Perhaps he will be duped, and we shall prevail over him,
And shall take our revenge on him"
But the Lord is with me as a dreaded warrior,
Therefore my persecutors shall stumble, and shall not prevail,
They shall be put to bitter shame, because they have not succeeded,
To everlasting confusion, which shall not be forgotten.[2]

Clearly one part of him would like to walk away from the whole thing. But there is another and even more powerful factor at work. Within him is the word of God. That word moves him to speak. He cannot stifle it—not because his freedom is taken away, but because he is enlivened by that word and to hold it in is like trying to contain a fire. From within, from the power of that word, comes the force that truly sets him free. He struggles against it, trying to be satisfied with less than that word demands—but, in his heart, he knows that happiness will come only in yielding to God. He has been called. He *is* a prophet. His actions must flow from this fact. To try to live in any other way is not just to disobey an order; it is to do violence to himself. It is self-destructive.

There is within us something that theologians have come to refer to as "natural law."[3] This does not mean that we have built into us a set of formalized legal statements. What it does mean is that along with the fact of what we are, there is discernible a pattern in the way in which we should live. Thinking about who and what we are leads us to realize that we must act in certain ways if we are to be faithful to ourselves. Of course, since we are God's creatures this also means that it is He who has made us what we are, and that in acting in the way proper to that identity we are being faithful not only to ourselves but to Him as well. Furthermore, theologians have come to the conclusion that this "natural law" would be part of us, even if there were no additional revelation of God. By the very fact that we are His human creatures there are certain obligations to Him and to each other that we could discover just by using our own intelligence. We might even add that to learn the basics of this natural law does not seem to require an excessive exercise of the mind. It may, in fact, appear to be almost instinctive in the way in which we learn to live with each other.

C.S. Lewis (referring to it as the Law of Nature) gives a very simple and thoroughly commonsense presentation of this in *Mere Christianity*. He writes:

Every one has heard people quarrelling. Sometimes it sounds funny and sometimes it sound merely unpleasant; but however it sounds, I believe we can learn something very important from listening to the kinds of things they say. They say things like this: "How'd you like it if anyone did the same to you?"—"That's my seat, I was there first"—"Leave him along, he isn't doing you any harm" . . . People say things like that every day, educated people as well as uneducated, and children as well as grown-ups.

Now what interests me about all these remarks is that the man who makes them is not merely saying that the other man's behaviour does not happen to please him. He is appealing to some kind of standard of behaviour which he expects the other man to know about. And the other man very seldom replies: "To hell with your standard." Nearly always he tries to make out that what he has been doing does not really go against the standard, or that if it does there is some special excuse.[4]

Lewis goes on to explain that there are certain standards of conduct which are found among all peoples at all times. He does not try to say that those standards have been put into practice in the same way in every instance, but that even when we find differences in practice we still see the same underlying norms. We do not find people with a *totally* different morality. It is impossible to find a society in which praise is heaped upon those who run away in time of danger, or where the source of pride is in our ability to turn in treachery upon those who love us most. They may differ, for example, in the way in which they express concern for family or tribe as opposed to outsiders, but there is general agreement on the fact that unselfishness is a virtue. Even those who attempt to deny the existence of this natural law will be the first to complain if you use some unfair tactic in arguing against them. Lewis goes on to say:

It seems, then, we are forced to believe in a real Right and Wrong. People may be sometimes mistaken about them, just as people sometimes get their sums wrong; but they are not a matter of mere taste and opinion any more than the multiplication table. Now if we are agreed about that, I go on to my next point, which is this. None of us are really keeping the Law of Nature. If there are any exceptions among you, I apologize to them. They had much better read some other work, for nothing I am going to saw concerns them. And now, turning to the ordinary human beings who are left:

I hope you will not misunderstand what I am going to say. I am not preaching, and Heaven knows I do not pretend to be better than anyone else. I am only trying to call attention to a fact; the fact that this year, or this month, or, more likely, this very day, we have failed to practice ourselves the kind of behaviour we expect from other people. There may be all sorts of excuses for us. That time you were so unfair to the children was when you were very tired. That slightly shady business about the money—the one you have almost forgotten—came when you were very hard up . . . That is to say, I do not succeed in keeping the Law of Nature very well, and the moment anyone tells me I am not keeping it, there starts up in my mind a string of excuses as long as your arm. The question at the moment is not whether they are good excuses. The point is that they are one more proof of how deeply, whether we like it or not, we believe in the Law of Nature . . . The truth is, we believe in decency so much—we feel the Rule of Law pressing on us so—that we cannot bear to face the fact that we are breaking it, and conse-quently we try to shift the responsibility. For you notice that it is only for our bad behaviour that we find all these explanations. It is only our bad temper that we put down to being tired or worried or hungry; we put our good temper down to ourselves.

These, then, are the two points I wanted to make. First, that human beings, all over the earth, have this curious idea that they ought to behave in a certain way and cannot really get rid of it. Secondly, that they do not in fact behave in that way. They know the Law of Nature; they break it. These two facts are the foundation of all clear thinking about ourselves and the universe we live in.[5]

The need for making moral decisions seems to come from what we are. Philosophers and theologians have spoken of our "nature" as the source of norms which govern our moral choices. What is the meaning of the word "nature"? To put it most simply, it answers the question, "What is this?" We might say, then, that once we are aware of what a thing is, we also have some insight, at least the beginnings of insight, into what it is for and what it can do. Frequently enough, when people speak of "natural law," they are referring to the kinds of norms that follow from an understanding of what we are as human beings. This easily leaves us with the impression that first we must analyze what we are, and then we can derive a set of rules about what we should do. There is some truth to this, but it is also a bit misleading to state it in this manner. It makes the whole thing sound quite theoretical, and our own experience tells us that this is not exactly the way it happens. Surely we should be able to think about and meditate upon our own nature, and this would lead us to a better understanding of the kinds of decisions we should make about our actions. But is that the way in which you came to the point of deciding that some things were right and others were wrong? As for myself, I would have to say that such a description would not be accurate.

As children we learn from others the distinctions between right and wrong. Some of those distinctions we simply accept because we trust the adults who teach us. As we mature we are increasingly able to think about what we have been taught and to make our decisions, not simply because we have been told something, but because we begin to understand the reasons for what we do. But in either case, whether we accept the authority of someone else or make a decision on the basis of our own knowledge, there is still something more involved. Why do we even think at all in terms of "right" and "wrong"? This is the question that is really at the heart of an understanding of natural law. Where does it all begin?

One of the best explanations that I have come across for this is given by Doctor Germain Grisez in his book, *The Way of the Lord Jesus,* Volume I. He points out that many theologians seem to begin by saying that there is, within us, a basic moral imperative that can be summarized as: "Do good and avoid evil." This would be the basic principle that would govern all of our actions, if we are really thinking about what we *ought* to do. But this, he suggests, is not actually the most basic source of our morality. It still leaves unanswered the more basic question: "*Why* should I do good and avoid evil?"

Saint Thomas Aquinas discusses what he calls the first principles of reason. Before we look at what he says about the first principle of practical reason (the principle upon which we base our idea of "natural law"), let's look at another sort of first principle. A first principle is supposed to be self-evident. This means that you do not have to prove it by forming arguments about it. Instead, you act upon it and are convinced of its truth even before you think about it. Once you do begin to think about it, you realize that it is indeed true and that it can never be proven to be false. For example, how do we know that our minds are capable of knowing the truth? I do not mean the truth of this or that particular thing, but simply the truth in general, the truth at all. Can we ever know the truth? To say that the mind is capable of knowing truth is self-evident. This means that we cannot prove it, but we can learn that every effort to deny it is doomed to failure.

Why can't we prove this? The answer to that is actually easy. Every time we set out to prove something, we use our minds. In this case it is the mind itself which is being questioned, so we cannot claim that we are proving our point by the use of the very thing we are discussing. On the other hand, we can actually know that we are able to grasp the truth. The way we go about getting some insight into this is to look, not at "proofs" that we offer, but at the reality of our own experience—an experience in which we come to realize that we can, indeed, know that something is true.

Suppose, for example, that someone says: "Human beings are never really able to know the truth." Well, once he says that, then that statement is either true or false. If it is false, then, of course, we can know the truth. If it is true, then, at least in this instance we can know the truth, so that statement must be false. This may sound complicated, but go through those first few sentences until you see what they really mean. They simply imply the fact that every time we claim that our minds are incapable of knowing any truth, we are actually experiencing the very opposite. We are really saying this: "Even though we may claim that we are incapable of knowing the truth, it is impossible for us to live with that statement." It is impossible even at a practical level. Once in a while you may meet someone who thinks that he is a complete skeptic. He is convinced of his position. He may argue with you about it. But in that process, he is undermining his own position. If one cannot ever know the truth, then why try to convince anyone of anything? It makes no sense. Even the skeptic cannot conduct his life on the basis of his own principle. If you ask him to give a lecture on his philosophy he will no doubt enter the lecture hall by the door—never for an instant doubting that it is there. He will actually deliver his lecture, not doubting the evidence of his senses that there is an audience there. He will gladly accept the check with which you pay him, he will cash it and he will be quite angry if it bounces. Time after time, he acts on the supposition that he can indeed know the truth.

This gives you an idea of what we mean by a first principle. It is not a question of something so difficult to prove that as a result no one can give you an argument for it. Rather, it is something so evident and obvious that there is no argument that can make it more obvious. Your own experience teaches you that you cannot live without it, and cannot really act against it.

In the moral area of our lives, there is also a first principle, which we may refer to as the first principle of practical reason. It is the principle which governs practice, which governs our actions. Saint Thomas had considerable insight into this. He did not state it as: "Do good and avoid evil." Instead, he states it in this way: "Good is to be done and pursued; what is evil is to be avoided."[6] How do these two statements differ? The first is really a moral rule. It is, in a sense, telling us to look at the objects of our actions. If they are good then we can perform the actions, if they are bad then we should avoid them. What Thomas says is more along these lines: "There is in us a basic instinct which moves us toward what we see as good and desirable. It is this which we find ourselves doing and pursuing. What we perceive as evil, we tend to avoid." We could also say that it means that we have within ourselves a tendency, which is part of our very nature, to seek our fulfillment. The "good" to which Thomas refers is not yet even describable as "moral good." It is simply the good which fulfills us as human beings. Again, it is a first principle, verified in our constant experience.

The principle which states that we are capable of knowing the truth, does not guarantee that everything we are capable of thinking is going to be true. It does not guarantee the truth of any particular thing. It merely states that we *can* know the truth. For any given instance, we shall have to examine the evidence and make a decision, knowing that we can, indeed, make mistakes. In the moral area as well, the mere fact that there is in us a tendency to seek our human fulfillment does not tell us that this act or that is truly fulfilling. Here, too, we are capable of error. But we have a starting point. We can begin to learn more and more about what it is that *truly* fulfills. We can learn from experience, we can learn from others. Note also that if we begin from the starting point of Saint Thomas, then we are not simply seeing morality as a set of positive and negative principles. Instead, we are beginning with the realization that the total thrust of our lives is toward the good. The whole movement is basically positive. We will certainly have to learn more specific facts by which to guide our conduct. We will, of necessity, learn to put these facts into concepts and words—which will assume the form of specific moral norms. But it is not simply a process of taking basic principles and from them deriving intellectual conclusions. Our thinking will always be in relation to our natural inclination to the good and things which fulfill those inclinations. This involves our experience.

As we more consciously choose to act for the good, and are more aware of how that good is to be found in particular instances, we are correspondingly more aware of the possibilities in our lives. This means that nature and natural-law morality have two aspects to be considered. There is both stability and change. Grisez says of natural-law morality that it is:

> Stable, in that the giveness and fundamental unalterability of natural inclinations account for the unalterability of the principles of natural law; but also changing, in that the dynamism of the inclinations, their openness to continuing and expanding fulfillment, accounts for the openness of natural law to authentic development.[7]

We have spoken of a "thrust" toward the good. We can actually be more specific in terms of categories of good toward which we are drawn. These goods can be categorized as seven in number:

> In sum, there are seven categories of basic human goods which perfect persons and contribute to their fulfillment both as individuals and in communities. Four of these can be called "reflexive," since they are both reasons for choosing and are in part defined in terms of choosing. These are: (1) self integration, which is harmony among all the parts of a person which can be engaged in freely chosen action; (2) practical reasonableness or authenticity, which is harmony among moral reflection, free choices, and their execution; (3) justice and friendship, which are aspects of the interpersonal communion of good persons freely choosing to act in harmony with one another; and (4) religion or holiness, which is harmony with God, found in the agreement of human individual and communal free choices with God's will. The reflexive goods also can be called "existential" or "moral," since they fulfill human subjects and interpersonal groups in the existential dimension of their being. The other three categories of basic human goods fulfill persons in the other three dimensions of their being. These goods can be called "nonreflexive" or "substantive," since they are not defined in terms of choosing, and they provide reasons for choosing which can stand by themselves. These are: (1) life itself, including health, physical integrity, safety, and the handing on of life to new persons; (2) knowledge of various forms of truth and appreciation of various forms of beauty or excellence; and (3) activities of skillful work and of play, which in their very performance enrich those who do them.[8]

When, therefore, we speak of human nature and natural law, we are not implying a static or abstract reality. This is one of the ways in which the classical moral theology sometimes was misleading. By beginning with a principle stated as: "Do good and avoid evil," and then proceeding to speak of this and all further norms as derived from human nature, theologians created an impression of a static, intellectualized moral sphere. The concept of human nature is actually dynamic, and so, too, is the concept of natural law. Doctor Grisez has a statement about this which is especially good, since it takes into account a wide range of the realities included in human nature. He writes:

> The human nature which is a standard for morality is not a formal essence and set of invariant relationships, as was suggested by the inadequate, scholastic natural-law theory. Rather the standard is the basic possibilities of human individuals as bodily creatures, endowed with intelligence, able to engage in fruitful work and creative play, physically complex, capable of more or less completely reasonable action, in need of companionship, capable of love, and open to friendship with God in whose image they are made.[9]

On the basis of all that has been said, what, then, follows? It follows that this thrust toward the good—the thrust to the attainment of the basic human goods—will result in the living of a life with moral norms. The thrust toward the good involves the use of our freedom. If we are freely to seek our fulfillment, then we should be choosing those things which are in conformity with human fulfillment. To choose otherwise would be folly. It would be self-destructive, precisely as was already indicated in an earlier chapter in reference to an understanding of sinfulness. When we speak, then, of natural law and come to the point of specifying particular acts as good or evil, we are acting on these basic principles and attempting to see how they are either verified or not in specific instances.

Why, you may be wondering, was this chapter entitled "Man and Superman"? On the other hand, you may not have wondered about that at all. In either case, prepare yourself, because I now intend to explain it. It has nothing to do with Clark Kent or the Man of Steel. It has to do, instead, with each and every one of us.

Up to this point in the chapter I have been speaking of human nature and natural law. But we are, in reality, more than human nature of itself would seem to imply; and the law by which we live is more than natural. Through God's revelation and our redemption in Christ we are now *supernatural*. We are called not only to human fulfillment in our goal of natural good; rather, we are called to a fulfillment which is to be found in our vocation of life in the Trinity.

To say that we are supernatural does *not* mean that nature has ceased to exist, nor does it mean that we are no longer natural. It is again a question that can be seen in the light of what I spoke of earlier as transposition. All that we are by nature remains with us; but we are, at the same time, even more. Sometimes people seem to speak of the natural and supernatural as though they were two levels of human existence, almost as though the image they had in mind was that of two layers of a cake. This is unfortunate, because it creates an understanding which is quite static. It makes a separation between natural and supernatural which ought not exist. It is not as though a new "level" is added to mankind. Rather it is as though the whole of his nature has been drawn to a new way of being and acting. Every act now has a dimension that it did not have by means of nature alone. We saw an example of this in speaking of the Eucharist. This is ingesting of nutrients, but with a totally new dimension. It becomes something quite new without ceasing to be what it was formerly. So, too, should we envision the relationship between nature and supernature. It involves a real transformation of our humanity, without any loss of what it was already.

This means also that all facets of natural law remain with us in our union with Christ. The supernatural builds on nature, it does not do away with it. A new relationship with God and neighbor is transposed into the old. This is one of the areas in which the ancient Gnostics went so wrong. They discounted nature, which they saw as body, and replaced it with spirit, which they saw as the new reality, the supernature. It was as though biology had been abandoned in favor of spirituality. Nothing could be further from the truth. In the supernatural it is still the *whole* person who must be fulfilled.

This means that both our spiritual and our biological needs are to be taken into account in this process of moral decision making. There have been theologians in the present day who have spoken against what they called "physicalism" or "biologism."[10] They were referring to what they saw as a tendency to explain morality on the basis of biological functions. For example, they would say that human sexuality in its biological dimension is procreative and that moral theologians placed too much weight on this biological aspect when they explained the morality of human sexuality. Those who oppose "physicalism" would then tend to explain human sexuality more in terms of the spiritual and psychological needs of the person, and could easily explain these in such a way as to imply that those needs could be met even while there was a conscious choice to frustrate the biological aspects of our actions. This sort of approach is, in my opinion, not totally removed from the old Gnosticism. It sees the psychological or spiritual needs of the person as taking precedence over the biological, and then concludes that this means that we can act rightly in such a way as to thwart the biological in favor of the higher needs. The proper view of the relationship between our needs will, indeed, give priority to the spiritual. But it will take into account that the spiritual does not do away with the other. Rather than removing a dimension, it gives new meaning to the lower dimensions. The biological needs remain, but they have now an even deeper meaning than before. Just as the Eucharist did not do away with ingestion of nutrients, but drew it into itself and added another dimension, so too can we see this in such areas of human sexuality. To act in such a way as to separate the needs and remove one in favor of another is really to act against that human integrity which is itself one of the basic goods. The realm of the supernatural elevates and gives new meaning to the natural; it does not eliminate it.

I am emphasizing this for a particular reason. It is because I want also to point out one final thing before I conclude this chapter. The Church approaches morality from the starting point of faith. For this reason some have contended that the Church cannot then make determinations about the natural law morality, since this is a matter of reason and not of faith. This is also a serious error. The Church not only can make such determinations; it is obliged to do so. The supernatural does not do away with the natural; it assumes it and transforms it. The natural goods of humanity remain. They now have, however, the added dimension that is to be found in union with Christ leading us into the life of the Trinity. To say that the Church can speak to the spiritual or the supernatural but not to the natural is to say that the two are simply coexisting but not interpenetrating, and this is simply wrong. The natural has been drawn into a new world, somewhat like the hypothetical fish I spoke of earlier. There is in reality a new vision—a vision with which we must see all reality if we are to attain to the fullness of salvation. The vision of the Church is indeed the vision of Christ, and it is a vision which see *all* reality in a new way and it must address that reality. This means also that the theologian, in realizing that the data for his study and exposition of any theological position must be drawn from the teaching and tradition of the Church, must also take into account the fact that the Church can and does speak in reference to and explanation of natural law. This, however, I shall consider further in the next chapter.

Notes

[1] Cf. Jer 1,4–10.

[2] Jer 20,7–11.

[3] What one might call the "classical" form of presentation of this concept of natural law can be found in any of the moral theology manuals. A much better presentation can be found in Germain Grisez, *The Way of the Lord Jesus*, Volume I: Christian Moral Principles, Chicago, 1983, pp. 103–106, 173–204. In the text I have made use of Doctor Grisez's ideas and I wish to give him credit for what I have said there. At the same time, I have to some extent abbreviated and refashioned what he has written, so I also want to acknowledge my own responsibility for ways in which my statements may not be either as complete or as exact as are his.

[4] C.S. Lewis, *Mere Christianity*, p. 17.

[5] *Ibid*, pp. 20–21.

[6] S.Th. I–II, q. 94, a. 2: "Et ideo primum principium in ratione parctica est, quod fundatur supra rationem boni, quae est: *Bonum est quod omnia appetunt*. Hoc est ergo primum praeceptum legis, quod bonum est faciendum et prosequendum, et malum vitandum."

[7] Grisez, *op.cit.*, p. 182.

[8] *Ibid*, p. 124.

[9] *Ibid*, p. 183.

[10] Cf., for example, Benedict M. Ashley, O.P., and Kevin D. O'Rourke, O.P., *Health Care Ethics: A Theological Analysis*, CHA, St. Louis, Second Edition, 1982, p. 34. They refer there to a number of authors who speak against "physicalism."

Chapter 8

Theology and Authority

During the afternoon of July 1, 1863, General Francis C. Barlow was engaged in heavy fighting just north of the town of Gettysburg. With his brigade of the Union's Eleventh Corps, he was attempting to stem the tide of the initial Confederate onslaught. Suddenly a musket ball struck his left side just near his spine. He attempted to walk away, but fell instead to the ground. Pressure from the Confederates forced Barlow's men back towards the town, leaving him behind. Shortly afterwards he was found by Confederate General John B. Gordon. By this time his arms and legs were paralyzed and he seemed at the point of death. Gordon spoke to him, gave him some water from his canteen, made him as comfortable as he could and then left, since there seemed nothing else that anyone could do. He did not die—at least not then. A few days later he was discovered by Union troops. In fact, he recovered from the wound, returned eventually to the army and went on, finally, to outlive many others who played a part in the Civil War.[1] I recall reading (although I cannot now recall the source) that one of his contemporaries commented that his miraculous recovery could probably be attributed to the fact that he had not been found in time for the doctors to treat him!

The Civil War era was a time of great optimism about man's progress and the state of his scientific knowledge. It is amusing now to go back and read the comments of those who could at that time hardly imagine what still might remain to be learned. What weapons could be more fearsome than the Gatling gun? What energy greater than the power of steam? What communication faster and better than the telegraph? Yet, whoever commented that Barlow was better off without medical assistance was probably absolutely right. What seemed then to be tremendous medical progress was as far from today's medicine as were all those other "never to be surpassed" Nineteenth Century achievements from their modern successors. Cleanliness in medical practice still meant wiping the saws and scalpels on a dirty apron before using them on the next patient. Operations without anaesthesia were often more of a shock to the body than was the illness they were intended to heal. The least treatment was most often the best.

At the time of the Civil War there were moralists commenting on ethical problems related to the practice of medicine. There were commentators long before then, and there have been such ever since. It is one area in the study of morality where we can see definite and clear development. It is for this reason that I chose to begin this chapter as I did. Moralists have long spoken of the obligation that we have to take care of our health. This obligation arises from the sacredness of life as a gift of God; just as we have an obligation to care for the lives of others, so must we also care for our own. This is seen to include the use of the proper means to preserve and foster our own good health. In the case of illness or accident, this would mean that we have a moral obligation to make some effort to rectify what may be a threat to our own lives. At the same time, moralists have realized that we cannot reasonably be expected to do *everything* that might be possible to preserve health. For example, one could not be held bound to make use of a treatment that was excessively painful and also held out little chance of success.[2]

The basic principle is stated along these lines: "One is bound to use the ordinary means of preserving health, but is not bound to use extraordinary means." While free to use extraordinary means, we are not obliged to do so. But then there arises an obvious question. What means are to be classified as extraordinary? Here the history of moral theology reveals a clear and definite development. From the Sixteenth to the Nineteenth Centuries, authors used examples such as the amputation of a leg or an abdominal operation. They spoke of intense, perhaps unbearable, pain and concluded that no one is morally bound to undergo this. They pointed to the maiming effects of amputation and the dreadful difficulty of living with its results. But in the Nineteenth Century the use of anaesthesia began. Eventually prostheses were developed. The use of antiseptics removed the high risk of deadly infection after surgery. In our own time, moralists would concur that most surgical procedures which are commonly performed would not carry with them the intensity of pain nor the seriousness of risk to life. They would now speak of such procedures as ordinary. In other words, the very same procedures which were extraordinary in one age came to be ordinary in another.

Did this mean that basic principles had to be changed? Not at all! In fact, the decision as to what constituted ordinary and extraordinary means was founded in those principles. In 1957 Pope Pius XII addressed this:

> Natural reason and Christian morals say that man (and whoever is entrusted with the task of taking care of his fellowman) has the right and duty in case of serious illness to take the necessary treatment for the preservation of life and health. This duty that one has toward himself, toward God, toward the human community, and in most cases toward certain determined persons, derives from a well-ordered charity, from submission to the Creator, from social justice and even from strict justice as well as from devotion toward one's family...
>
> But normally one is held to use only ordinary means—according to the circumstances of persons, places, times and cultures—that is to say, means that do not involve any grave burdens for oneself or another. *A more strict obligation would be too burdensome for most men and would render the attainment of a higher, more important good too difficult. Life, health, all temporary activities are in fact subordinated to spiritual ends.* On the other hand, one is not forbidden to take more than the strictly necessary steps to preserve life and health, as long as he does not fail in some more serious duty.[3]

Here we have a perfect example of a basic norm being applied to differing situations. In each case the results are somewhat different, yet the same norm is applicable and consistent. Furthermore, it is spelled out in an official, authoritative form in papal teaching, but even that does not mean that the application will ever after be cast in stone. Since the time of Pius XII there have tremendous advances in medical procedures and techniques—changes that could probably not have been envisioned in 1957 when Pius XII spoke on the topic. Yet the statement that he made is as readily applicable now as it was then.

This example contains a number of elements worthy of serious consideration. First of all, it is a clear instance of development in the application of moral norms and in the refinement of our grasp of them. Even though the norms are the same, changing circumstances make us realize that their implications are different. Secondly, it is an example of a situation in which official teaching authority in the Church and the work of theologians progress together, mutually complementing one another. This is what we should hope, ideally, to find in the living of the life of the Body of Christ. Growth in theological knowledge, arrived at by means of a great deal of discussion and argumentation, is brought to a level at which it finds confirmation and expression in the official teaching of the Church. Thirdly, it is clear that the official teaching makes no claim to solve all practical problems for the future. The norms are spelled out clearly, but they will still have to be applied in accord with procedures that cannot be envisioned in advance. Yet the principle remains. Fourthly, the statement of the Pope, while confirming a principle underlying moral decisions, also implies the wrongness of the opposite position. Were one to say that we are obliged to undergo all possible means of treatment, without regard for pain or expense or possibly disappointing results, he would be running counter to general theological consensus and to papal teaching. This is, in fact, what is taken into account at the present time in the very serious discussions about particular cases in which one is morally justified in refusing further treatment as the approach of death becomes increasingly imminent. Finally, it is noteworthy that the statement by the Pope does not at all prohibit further theological work and understanding. In fact, it would seem to encourage it, since this norm must constantly be applied to newly evolving situations.

I have purposely chosen a rather "peaceful" example. There are other areas in theology, especially in moral theology, where that same peace might not be found. The present age has, for example, become much more aware of areas of social justice that must be addressed from a moral perspective. There are questions about such things as a "just war" and what this means in the current context of atomic weaponry. One can hardly look back to preceding Church teaching and expect to find there all the answers to such inquiries. There may, indeed, be lines of thought that are already present, but the particulars of modern life may have to be thoroughly examined in order to arrive at solutions to moral dilemmas. From this, eventually, an increasingly deepened sense of Christian morality can emerge and can begin to assume the form of clear teaching for the better formation of conscience. There are also currently a number of moral issues which are widely publicized, and in which there seems to be considerable dispute. At the focal point of that dispute is the question of the relationship between the teaching duties of theologians and the proper use of authority in the Church. Before we look at this specifically, however, it would be well to speak of authority in a more general perspective. This is what I shall do in the next few pages.[4]

Lumen Gentium is the name of the Second Vatican Council's Dogmatic Constitution on the Church, issued on 21 November 1964. Within the third chapter of this document is a much quoted section (n. 25). So as to avoid having too many lengthy quotations here in the chapter, I have given the full text of this passage in an appendix. It would be well, then, for you to refresh your memory of it and then return to the reading of this chapter.

Having reviewed the text, then let's look at what it means. First of all, it is worthy of note that the claims made in this passage are not anything more than what we would expect on the basis of the concepts that Cardinal Newman had presented, and which we examined in an earlier chapter. Underlying the whole passage is the realization that if the Church is to be able to proclaim its faith, then there must be those in the Church capable of doing so with authority. This follows from the fact that we are dealing with revelation and faith, and we are not simply concerned with items that can be established upon the basis of reason alone. Acceptance in faith *always* implies authority, since we accept something as true on the word of someone else. In matters of faith, that authority is ultimately on the authority of God revealing Himself to us. But that revelation comes to us in and through a living community, the Church.

From the earliest times—as, again, we have already seen—the authentic leaders of the community have been the bishops and their teaching has been viewed as normative for the faith of Christians. To conjecture, then, that the Church is capable of accepting revelation in faith, and then to say that those who teach that faith to and in the name of the whole Church are, at least in their totality, capable of error in such essentials, is thoroughly unthinkable. But why would it be unthinkable? Because of the peculiar nature of that with which we are dealing. We are considering a reality within the framework of our union with Christ, a union which has been described in terms of the Body of Christ, and which is essential for our salvation. It is not just a matter of abstract truths presented for our consideration, but of truths that are the root of God's gift of salvation. This is also why the document speaks of "faith and morals." We are concerned with a whole way of life and with the fact that this way of life is God's gift to us and we have *His* assurance that it is being truly communicated. In other words, we are speaking of a charism, a freely given grace of God, which it makes perfect sense to expect to find in His Church.

We have also seen that the position occupied by the Pope is unique in the Church. The growing self-understanding of the Church included not only the leadership of the bishops, but that of the Bishop of Rome in particular. He is and has been viewed as occupying a position which includes the function of authentic, authoritative teaching in the name of the Church. He is capable of expressing its faith in terms of doctrine and life—faith and morals. It was on this ground that there finally emerged, in the First Vatican Council more than a century ago, the statement on the infallibility of the Pope. Vatican II actually does little more in reference to the Pope than to repeat that same statement. It has, however, placed it even more clearly in its relationship to the teaching authority of all the bishops as a whole.

If you examine the statements of the First Vatican Council and the Second Vatican Council as well, you find that this concept of infallibility in reference to bishops and Pope is not presented in such a way as to somehow separate them from the rest of the Church. Rather, the charism belongs to the Church as a whole. It is that Church, infallible in its faith, which has its authentic leaders—leaders who must be able to exercise that charism. If we attempt to understand this simply as though we were dealing with a description of some legal right or other, we would find it difficult indeed to specify just what we meant. Instead, we must be sure that we keep it within the context of a living Church, the Body of Christ. Within this frame of reference we can begin to grasp the proper interrelationship of the members. We can also see that what makes sense in terms of reasonability can also be grasped much more deeply in terms of what we have described as transposition. That which makes sense even at a purely human level makes all the more sense when we realize that we are here dealing with God's grace. Common sense (I think) and experience (I am certain) conspire to teach us that this infallibility of the Church does not extend in the same way to each and every individual member of the Body, but that it is to be found in the *whole* body and in specific ways in specific members.

We should note that the teaching of the Church is rather restrained in terms of its description of the extent of such infallibility. There is certainly no claim that everything taught by the Church is infallible. Here again it would seem clear that the Church's growing self-awareness has played its essential role. There are times when final and definitive answers to questions of faith are required. There are also times when the Church's consciousness of the implications of its faith is still in process, and no definitive answer can yet be given. There is clearly no idea of some sort of secret stock of answers from which teaching authority can draw in time of need. It is equally evident that the Church does not rely on some sort of "new" revelation to fill its needs. Always the teaching of the Church is itself governed by what it has already received and learned and taught. In other words, the Church does not "create" its revelation; instead, it is governed by what it has been given in and through the person of Jesus, the revealing Word of the Father. What the Church is saying about itself is at least this: There is no claim of having all the answers to all the questions that can ever arise; but there is an assurance that the Magisterium (teaching authority) in the Church will not and cannot lead the Church astray in its faith or in its mode of living.

Members of the Church will, of course, assent to what the Church teaches. But such assent can imply a variety of levels of acceptance. The most eminent of these levels is the full and total acceptance in faith that is demanded by an infallible statement. *Lumen Gentium* outlines the ways in which such a statement can come about. The clearest instances are those which arise from the "extraordinary" exercise of teaching authority. The Pope, acting in his position as supreme pastor and teacher of the Church, can proclaim an absolute decision in a teaching pertaining to faith and morals. This the Church is solemnly bound to accept. Note carefully that the conditions for such a statement are quite limited. It is a matter of faith and morals, it is a matter which is clearly being defined and it is done by the Pope, not simply as an individual teacher, but in the exercise of his highest office. The second form of extraordinary exercise of teaching authority comes from an ecumenical council. Again, there are conditions which must be met. We would be much mistaken if we were to think that everything that a Council says is to be taken as a matter of faith. Rather, the Council must clearly be teaching in the area of faith and morals, and it must be clearly intending to define something. Both the Pope and the Councils are capable of teaching in a variety of ways that are not considered as definitions. In fact, the bulk of papal and conciliar teaching over the centuries would not fall into this category of the infallible. This is precisely why it is described as extraordinary—it is rather unusual.

Along with such extraordinary teaching there is what is referred to as the ordinary teaching of Pope or bishops. This is the day to day teaching activity that is an essential part of the office of the pastor. Even here there are certain conditions under which such teaching can be considered infallible. When the bishops, even spread throughout the world and not gathered in Council, teach authoritatively, in union with the Pope, that some matter of faith and morals is to be definitively held as part of the Christian faith—under these conditions their teaching is to be considered infallible. Note what all three cases have in common: Papal definitions, Conciliar definitions and this particular exercise of ordinary teaching authority all deal clearly and decisively with matters of faith and morals. To say that, under such conditions, the Pope and bishops could be in error would be to say that those who have the responsibility to teach the faith are not able to do so. In other words, these conditions make it clear that we are dealing with a kind of teaching that should bind all the faithful to acceptance. The bond is not simply a legal norm, but is founded quite obviously in the unity of Christians in the living Body of Christ.

We should note another essential item as well: When the Pope or a Council exercises such teaching authority, we can discover that clearly enough from the way in which it is done. The documents indicate that this is what is happening. Of course, we still have to be very careful to study the documents as deeply as we can in order to be quite clear about what precisely is being taught. We may find some greater difficulty in the area where the ordinary magisterium of bishops in union with the Pope is being exercised infallibly. Here we have no single document upon which we can rely. Instead, such a position might have to be established on the basis of considerable study of a wide variety of documents. This, of course, can be accomplished, but it may involve much more work.

There still remains what is indeed the largest part of the teaching of the Church—teaching which does not fall into the narrower conditions outlined above for infallible teaching. Here, too, our assent is necessary, but it is not always the assent of faith. Instead, we may be dealing with various levels of assent, depending on the type of teaching and subject matter that is involved. The reality of our union with Christ in the Church should make us realize that in this instance there must be respect for the authority of those who teach and acceptance of what they teach. This sort of acceptance is described in *Lumen Gentium*. It is made clear that the individual bishops do not enjoy the privilege of infallibility. Yet it says:

> Bishops who teach in communion with the Roman Pontiff are to be revered by all as witnesses of divine and Catholic truth; the faithful, for their part, are obliged to submit to their bishop's decision, made in the name of Christ, in matters of faith and morals, and to adhere to it with a ready and respectful allegiance of mind.

The implication here is certainly not that every matter in which the bishop proposes teaching on faith or morals is to be taken as an item of faith. But it does imply that there is need for respect as well as assent to the overall teaching of the bishop. It does not mean that the bishop cannot be wrong; but it implies that the fact of his union with his fellow bishops and the bishop of Rome is an indication of his trustworthiness in teaching.

The position of the Pope is described also in terms of his ordinary teaching. In this respect the document says:

> This loyal submission of the will and intellect must be given, in a special way, to the authentic teaching authority of the Roman Pontiff, even when he does not speak *ex cathedra* in such wise, indeed, that his supreme teaching authority be acknowledged with respect, and that one sincerely adhere to decisions made by him, conformably with his manifest mind and intention, which is made known principally either by the character of the documents in question, or by the frequency with which a certain doctrine is proposed, or by the manner in which the doctrine is formulated.

I referred a bit earlier to current disputes about the relationship between the teaching duties of theologians and the proper use of authority in the Church. A good deal of this discussion centers on the meaning of the preceding paragraph. We are clearly dealing with a type of papal teaching that is not being put into the form of infallible proclamation. What does this mean? As I already indicated, the presence of teaching authority in the Church does *not* mean that there is some secret store of answers to every possible doctrinal and moral question that can arise. In fact, what happens in the course of the history of the Church is that questions which come up are given response in a way that usually clearly reflects the reality of development as we have already seen it. Answers may at first be tentative; theologians begin to respond on the basis of knowledge already available. In moral situations the responses will be founded in principles already developed, and such answers may clearly point to the need for reformulation of principles. Official statements of the Pope, dealing with such cases, will reflect the indecision still present. They may also appear tentative and in succeeding statements may be gradually clarified. The norms involved in this process, however, are more than simply the norms of growth in human understanding. By this I mean that it is not simply a process of rationalism pure and simple. Instead, the truth of the matter will always have to take into account the previous teaching of the Church, because the living tradition is one of the sources of resolution to current questions. What we are dealing with is a growing self-awareness of the Church, and not merely theoretical concepts. Theories proposed by theologians always have to be balanced against the experience of the Church as expressed in and through its Magisterium.

The need for reformulation of teaching can arise from the fact that every human effort to express the truth is a *human* effort. As such it can easily be incomplete and even the obvious sense of the words may not, in a given instance, fully express what the speaker wishes to say. Ford and Kelly, as far back as 1958, presented an interesting example of this possibility. They spoke about the statements of Pius XI and Pius XII in regard to sterilization in general and the question of punitive sterilization:

> In the originally published text of *Casti Connubii,* the words of Pius XI at least strongly implied that he was condemning punitive sterilization; but a *notandum* in the next fascicle of the *Acta apostolicae sedis* contained a rewording of the passage which showed that the Pope did not intend to commit himself on the controversy among theologians about the licitness of punitive sterilization. Ten years later the Holy Office, with the approval of Pius XII, condemned direct sterilization, without qualification, as being contrary to the natural law. That was in 1940. But in 1951, and again in 1953, Pope Pius XII, when referring to this condemnation, restricted it to the direct sterilization of the innocent. In both these instances, the Popes apparently realized that, though perfectly apt for condemning the errors at which they were aimed, the formulas were broader than their own intention.[5]

Here we have an example of the Popes themselves making corrections to earlier statements. From this Ford and Kelly conclude:

> The very fact that Popes themselves have gone out of their way to clarify or restrict their moral pronouncements indicates that a theologian in not necessarily irreverent or disloyal in supposing that other such statements may need clarification or restriction or rephrasing.[6]

Part of the function of the theologian is to interpret documents of the Church, including papal statements, and to bring their meaning to bear upon the study of theology. Such interpretation must also take into account both context and intent. Again, Ford and Kelly write:

> From the foregoing it follows that the words alone do not always give us the sense, the true meaning, of a papal pronouncement. To get to the true sense, the theologian must study not only the words, but their context and the papal intention in making the pronouncement. By the context we mean not so much the verbal context as the historical setting, because it is there particularly that we are apt to find the true meaning of the statement. For example, if

the Pope is settling a controversy, his words should be taken in conjunction with the controversy; if he is condemning an error, the words should be interpreted in reference to the error and so forth.[7]

Here we see that papal statements can be corrected later, and that the Popes themselves have done so. We also see that theologians have an obligation to examine all data, including papal statements, carefully and interpret such data properly. Furthermore, proper interpretation and understanding may lead the theologian to see the need for correction. It would be quite proper for him then to point this out and to make use of this realization in his further studies.

The problems of the present time, however, go quite a bit further than what is indicated in the last few paragraphs. What had once been a question of the realization of a need for correction and a rather respectful intention to make such correction has been put more recently into terms of "dissent" from non-infallible papal teaching. This may not seem to some to be much of a difference; in my opinion it is a very serious difference. An aura seems to have been created of a wide gap between infallible and non-infallible papal teaching—a sort of gap that creates the impression that the former must be accepted while the latter has little or no real authority. It creates the very narrow mind-set of a kind of legalism: If it's not defined, then I can take it or leave it. It creates the utterly false impression that defined doctrine requires assent, while all else is mere opinion from which one can dissent at will. This is clearly quite far removed from what we have already seen in preceding chapters about the teaching function of the Church. It is not simply a legal organization imposing rules and tenets of faith. It is the living Body of Christ, proclaiming God's revelation and bringing that word to life in its continuing history. Times of crisis may demand clear definition, but most times demand honest teaching with good-willed and willing acceptance.

The relevant paragraph in *Lumen Gentium* itself contains a clear expression of the awareness of a variety of levels of adherence to differing sorts of statements, and it even contains certain criteria to help determine that. But there still remains the fact that such teaching must be taken very seriously indeed. In 1984, speaking in Dallas, Cardinal Ratzinger addressed this same issue:

> As I said in my opening talk, the teaching of the Council on the levels of assent is very important for us here. *Lumen Gentium*, paragraph twenty-five, gives *three* criteria for deciding: the *character* of the document, the *frequency* of repetition of the teaching, and the *manner* of speaking. It is clear that the Church teaches in various forms of seriousness. The decrees of a legitimate Council, papal definitions and encyclicals all differ and have a clear history of development which must be considered if they are to be interpreted correctly. When the Church teaches something continually, that is more important than something she has taught only occasionally, or has ceased to emphasize at all. Finally, the document

itself will reveal diverse manners of speaking within the same composition. Not every concept in a papal document of definition is being defined infallibly. It seems to me that this distinction will help a great deal. If I say that the position of the Church against artificial contraception has had a continuous history for the last fifty years, it simply *cannot* be maintained that it is a position of no consequence and less importance. Further, to make the observation that a particular statement is not infallible is not all that helpful, especially if the statement itself never pretended to be so. Just because a statement is not in the most solemn form possible, it is not rendered theologically insignificant to serious Catholic theological study.[8]

There have always been those who have rejected the teaching of the Church's Magisterium. This is clear enough even in the short summary of events given above in the chapter on the early Church. There has also been consistently an awareness of the need for continued development and its attendant need for amplification and correction of preceding documents and positions. None of this is particularly surprising. What seems to be different at the present time is the fact that a number of theologians are the ones who speak most decidedly about "dissent." This creates an apparent rift between theology and Magisterium, and it is this which for many is the most disturbing bone of contention in our own day. A good deal of this, in fact, stems back to the time of controversy following the promulgation of the Encyclical, *Humanae Vitae*, of Pope Paul VI. Even before that, however, at the First Synod of Bishops in 1967, there was concern about the relationship of theologians and Magisterium, and this seems to have to some extent been responsible for the request of those bishops that the Pope appoint a theological commission. Paul VI did appoint an International Theological Commission in 1969 and it held its first meeting in that year and has continued to meet since then. It was at its meeting in 1975 that it prepared a document entitled *Theses on the Relationship Between the Ecclesiastical Magisterium and Theology*.[9] The composition of the Commission was such as to be widely representative of theologians throughout the world, and the publication of its statement is an indication of its approval by the Congregation for the Doctrine of the Faith.[10]

The *Theses* begin with the awareness of a need to clarify the relationship between Magisterium and theology. The Magisterium is viewed as having the task of protecting divine revelation, while the task of the theologian is the investigation and explanation of the doctrine of the faith. The second, third and fourth of the twelve theses deal with elements common to both Magisterium and theologians in exercising their proper tasks. Both are seen as being in service to the people of God and both share (each in its own way) in preserving the deposit of revelation as well as examining, explaining, teaching and defending it. Neither Magisterium nor theology is viewed as operating in a way totally free of restriction. Both are bound to limits set by the fact of revelation and its continued existence in this world. They are thus bound by the word of God itself, never being above it but always in service to it. They are bound also by the Church's own sense of its faith as this has been expressed in the past and present. This sense or appreciation of its faith is seen as rising from the fact that there is indeed a living community extended in both time and space. Likewise, Magisterium and theology are both bound by the documents of tradition which set forth that faith. Finally, both are bound by the pastoral and missionary concern which is at the heart of the task of the Church. The common purpose and common limits of Magisterium and theology should result in an awareness of the need for a co-responsible, cooperative and collegial enterprise. The members of the Magisterium and theologians should act with an appreciation of the need for joint effort.

While one can speak of common elements and common goals, there are also differences that should be clearly noted. These are dealt with in theses five through eight. The theses indicate four areas of difference: (1) Function, (2) quality of authority, (3) connection with the Church and (4) proper freedom and critical function. It would be worthwhile to look, even briefly, at each of these.

The *first* difference refers to the fact that the task of the Magisterium is to defend the integrity and unity of faith and morals. This can create a vision that looks somewhat negative, as though the function could be defined simply in terms of rejection of error. In fact, it also includes the positive teaching role of the Magisterium. The function of theologians is envisioned as in some way mediating between Magisterium and people of God. It draws together the faith of the universal Church and the discoveries of science, history and philosophy. At the same time, theology acts to interpret and translate into contemporary modes of thought both the teachings and the warnings of the Magisterium.

The *second* difference is found in the awareness that magisterial authority is based in ordination and is a "formal authority," both charismatic and juridical. Theologians have an authority that comes from their scientific qualifications. At the same time the theses point out a certain mutuality. In reference to magisterial authority they say: "Care should be taken that personal authority and the authority that derives from the very matter being proposed also be brought to bear when this magisterial authority is being put into effect." In other words, there should not be the simple exercise of an "official" authority without the personal example and clarity of presentation that ought to be present as well. On the other hand, theologians are not authoritative in a purely scientific sense. They are dealing with a "science of faith" and this cannot be put into practice without both the lived experience and practice of their own faith.

The *third* difference is in their connection to the Church. Clearly, both Magisterium and theologians should work in and for the Church. The Magisterium, as a task conferred by sacred orders, is an institutional element in the Church focussed especially on pastoral concern—the leading and feeding of the flock entrusted to them. Any member of the Church can be involved in the task of theology insofar as that member is living the life of the Church and has the necessary competence of learning.

Finally, the *fourth* difference is in terms of the freedom proper to each and the critical function of each. Here the theses speak of freedom and responsibility for both Magisterium and theology. What is said is probably best quoted in full:

1. By its nature and institution, the magisterium is clearly free in carrying out its task. This freedom carries with it a great responsibility. For that reason, it is often difficult, although necessary, to use it in such a way that it not appear to theologians and to others of the faithful to be arbitrary or excessive. There are some theologians who prize scientific theology too highly, not taking enough account of the fact that respect for the magisterium is one of the specific elements of the science of theology. Besides, contemporary democratic sentiments often given rise to a movement of solidarity against what the magisterium does in carrying out its task of protecting the teaching of faith and morals from any harm. Still, it is necessary, though not easy, to find always a mode of procedure which is both free and forceful, yet not arbitrary or destructive of communion in the Church.

2. To the freedom of the magisterium there corresponds in its own way the freedom that derives from the true scientific responsibility of theologians. It is not an unlimited freedom, for, besides being bound to the truth, it is also true of theology that "in the use of any freedom, the moral principle of personal and social responsibility must be observed" [Vatican II, *Dignitatis Humanae,* n. 7]. But the theologians' task of interpreting the documents of the past and present magisterium, of putting them in the context of the whole of revealed truth, and of finding a better understanding of them by the use of hermeneutics brings with it a somewhat critical function which obviously should be exercised positively rather than destructively.

The ninth thesis reiterates what should be obvious at this point. In the exercise of the functions of Magisterium and theologians, there will at times be tension between them. Members of the hierarchy and theologians are all human—redeemed in Christ and still in process of arriving at the fullness of that redemption. The Church is alive, and life and growth involve tension. They warn, then, that tension should not be immediately interpreted as opposition or hostility. Rather, we must keep in mind that it is a sign of vital force.

The last three theses deal with how to promote the proper relationship between theologians and the Magisterium. The relationship is described as dialogue, and that dialogue is envisioned as being founded in community in the faith of the Church and service is building up the Church. The relationship is seen, in fact, as antecedent to any actual dialogue. The reality of dialogue, however, provides for the Magisterium a greater understanding of the faith it defends and preaches, while theological understanding gains from corroboration by the Magisterium. The limit on dialogue is set by the truth of faith, for it is this which must be served and explained. It is also quite clearly pointed out that this truth is not to be seen as something uncertain or utterly unknown, but as a truth revealed and handed on in the Church.

In the eleventh thesis there is a passage that refers to problems which interfere with dialogue. It reads:

> This goal of the dialogue, the service of the truth, is often endangered. The following types of behavior especially limit the possibility of dialogue: wherever the dialogue becomes an "instrument" for gaining some end "politically," that is, by applying pressure and ultimately abstracting from the question of truth, the effort is bound to fail; if a person "unilaterally" claims the whole field of the dialogue, he violates the rules of discussion; the dialogue between the magisterium and theologians is especially violated if the level of argument and discussion is prematurely abandoned and means of coercion, threat, and sanction are immediately brought to bear; the same thing holds when the discussion between theologians and the magisterium is carried out by means of publicity, whether within or outside the Church, which is not sufficiently expert in the matter, and these "pressures" from without have a great deal of influence, e.g. the mass media.

Finally, in the twelfth thesis, they speak of steps to be taken in the case of questions about the opinions of a theologian. Rather than begin with an official examination of a theologian's writings, authority is advised to exhaust the ordinary steps that might lead to a satisfactory resolution. Such steps would include personal conversation and inquiries and replies by correspondence. Only if such preliminary inquiries fail to produce a consensus is it necessary to proceed to such things as verbal sanctions or warnings. "In a very serious case, the magisterium— after consulting theologians of various schools and having exhausted the means of dialogue—for its part must necessarily clarify the compromised truth and safeguard the faith of believers."

The theses seem to represent a rather well balanced effort to explain the relationship between Magisterium and theology, as well as the possibilities of tension, dialogue and resolution of problems. The thought contained in the theses seems to be based in an awareness of our unity in the Body of Christ, along with the awareness of our own human limitations. Magisterium and theologians are both encouraged to accomplish their respective tasks and to avoid those things which would interfere either with their attainment of a deeper insight into the truths of faith or with the pastoral responsibilities entailed in the unfolding of those truths. As has already been noted often enough, that pastoral responsibility also includes the teaching and proclamation of a Christian way of life. It deals with morality as well as with doctrine.

I referred above to the problems that had arisen at the time of the Encyclical, *Humanae vitae*. I would like now to return to a brief consideration of that period. It seems to be rather evident that within the circumstances surrounding the issuing of that letter we can find a process which had, in fact, made dialogue exceedingly difficult if not impossible. It also seems possible that somewhat the same circumstances may be at work even at present.

In 1980 there appeared in *Homiletic and Pastoral Review* an article by James Hitchcock, in which he reviewed the events which preceded the publication of the encyclical. This article gives a clear summary of what happened in the period between 1964 and 1968 (the time of the encyclical) as far as the formation of public opinion was concerned. The article is well worth reading, and I would suggest that you do so. At present I will make use of some of its ideas, but in a much abbreviated form. There was growing speculation that the Church would in some way alter its stance on birth control. There was a papally appointed commission studying the question with a view to supplying information and conclusions to be used by the Pope. Many theologians were speculating not only the possibility of change, but on its inevitability as well. The Second Vatican Council, in its documents, had given no indication that any change was forthcoming. In fact, what it did say was in full accord with earlier teaching.[11] In its pastoral constitution on the Church in the modern world, *Gaudium et Spes* (n. 51), it said "In questions of birth regulation, the sons of the Church, faithful to these principles, are forbidden to use methods disapproved of by the teaching authority of the Church in its interpretation of the divine law."[12] The Council did not go further into the question, since it was to be studied by the papal commission in preparation for a more complete statement at a later time. It was during these same few years that the media began more increasingly to speak of the "Catholic ban" on birth control and its possible revision. This, together with the publicity given to theological speculations, set the stage for a great disappointment on the part of many in the face of *Humanae Vitae*.

The theses of the theological commission spoke of factors which can disrupt and destroy dialogue. Among them was a use of the communications media, which are not expert in theology and so can seriously distort the reality of what is happening. This factor was most definitely involved in the period preceding *Humanae Vitae*. I would also add another factor that can and must be taken into account in coverage given by the media. Not only is there a lack of expertise, there is also quite frequently a lack of any real understanding of the sorts of values that may be at stake. What makes a good story and sells papers may have little or nothing to do with a search for the truth or a desire to grasp the deepest meanings of morality. This is not to imply malice on the part of those who seek out and report news. It is merely recognition of the fact that the interests at work in reporting and those at work in theology and Church teaching are thoroughly different. We should be most careful indeed not to mistake one for the other.

The coverage in the press was an important factor in the divided reception of the encyclical. In one sense, however, it was unavoidable. The fact of any discussion within the Church on contraception was news. Theologians, exercising the right and duty to study and explain the faith, will and should be involved in speculation. If they are to communicate with each other, then much of that communication will probably take place in journals, lectures, meetings and conferences; and the results of such will generally be available for anyone who wishes to have access to them. It would be foolish to try to carry out the work of theology under some sort of heavy veil of secrecy. In other words, one cannot simply place blame on theologians for the fact that their work may be publicized or even misinterpreted. It is quite a different question, however, if the theologians themselves are purposely making use of publicity in order to create pressure. This is *not* a search for truth and it is *not* the proper carrying out of the function of the theologian. Rather, it is a signal of the end of real dialogue. Why? Because it is a sign that the theologian who does this has already made up his mind that he is right, and he is now attempting to use force to bring about acceptance of what he teaches—even though he may be claiming that what he says should be accepted on the merits of the arguments he proposes. When that sort of force is aimed at the Magisterium itself, it is, in my opinion, a serious breach of the trust and responsibility that should be part of the whole theological endeavor. But did any theologians do that? I think so, and my opinion is not based simply on fancy.

One of the theologians who was especially involved in the aftermath of the encyclical was Father Charles Curran of the Catholic University of America. In 1976 he wrote about the events of 1968 and the preceding years.[13] In his presentation he discusses both the motives for his own reaction to the encyclical and the means he chose to respond to it. This is important, because otherwise what I have to say about these might seem to be based on conjecture. He also discusses his own development as a theologian, in the course of which he speaks of his questioning of the teaching on contraception as early as 1964. He says:

> Shortly thereafter I became convinced of the need to change the teaching of the Roman Catholic Church on birth control and before the year was out wrote an article to explain my change and gave addresses on this topic.[14]

He goes on to give his own description of what happened after the encyclical. During the early part of 1968 there were signs that the Pope was not going to accept the position adopted by the majority of the commission studying contraception, and that he would issue some statement on it. Father Curran describes being out of Washington for the summer, but having contingency reservations to fly back. He describes his position before the issuing of the encyclical:

> We tried in vain to raise enough publicity to prevent the issuance
> of any encyclical. In my judgment an encyclical at that time reaf-
> firming the older teaching would be catastrophic. Many people
> would think that they could no longer be loyal Roman Catholics
> because of their decision to practice artificial contraception.
> Priests would be searching for guidance and would also be thrown
> into great crises of conscience. I was convinced that most Catholics
> and priests did not even know about the right to dissent from
> authoritative, noninfallible, hierarchical teaching. Plans then began
> to take shape to formulate a response to the encyclical which was
> rumored to be imminent.[15]

The decision was made to meet in Washington and there to plan a response
to the encyclical, copies of which were supposed to be available to the group by
then. About ten theologians met, read the encyclical and discussed a response.
Father Curran insisted that the response must contain a statement on the "question of dissent." They agreed to hold a press conference the next morning and by
then had obtained the agreement of a number of others by telephone. Father
Curran writes:

> Naturally this response received headline news throughout the
> United States and on all the television media. In fact we were able
> to hold subsequent press conferences in the next few days in an
> attempt to obtain as much coverage as possible.[16]

He says that this quick and forceful action, and its support by so many
theologians, was able to accomplish their purpose. In the next sentence he describes that purpose:

> The day after the encyclical was promulgated American Catholics
> could read in their morning papers about their right to dissent and
> the fact that Catholics could in theory and practice disagree with
> the papal teaching and still be loyal Roman Catholics.[17]

He goes on then to say that he *hopes* that for many Catholics this solved some
problems, but says also that he is *sure* that for many it created problems—that is,
for those who "could not understand this kind of dissent." He mentions also that
there were two false charges which "tended to ruffle me more than usual." These
were the claim, made by some, that those who dissented had never read the
encyclical, and the claim that their action was precipitous. He then states:

> As was to be expected, this organized dissent caused quite a stir in
> the Roman Catholic Church in the United States. Catholic Univer-

sity was the center of focus in the academic discussion because the core group had many members associated with the University, and I was recognized as the principal animator of the group.[18]

I would like now to look at some of the elements in this account. With a number of items I have serious and, I think, well-founded disagreement. I would also like to point out that what I am going to say is a matter of issues and not of personalities, nor should what I say be understood as directed toward Catholic University. The University is mentioned in the passages above simply because, in fact, Father Curran mentioned it and not because I have anything to say about it. Near the end of the chapter from which I have been quoting, Father Curran says:

> I realistically expect controversy and do not mind it . . . The somewhat vitriolic attacks in the conservative Catholic press and hate mail are things I can readily shrug off . . . Most of these problems never cause me any pain or anger, but rather I just keep on doing what I feel is right.[19]

I have no use for either vitriol or hate mail and I do not think that anyone needs to be subjected to either. I honestly admire the fact that Father Curran can shrug them off without anger or pain, and I have no intention of causing either. At the same time, I have, as I said, serious disagreement with what happened in 1968 and with some of the things that seem to be happening at present. I also think that it is right for me to point out what such disagreements are.

It is proper to speak of both change and development in theology and in the Church's teaching. This we have already seen. The teaching about birth control has been presented in Church documents as quite serious and of long standing. It is in such an area that we might expect to find outright change less likely, even though there is always room for development and refinement of the ways in which principles find concrete application. In fact, if one examines the documents from the time of Pius XI to that of John Paul II, a development is clear. Earlier statements about birth control can give one the impression the even family planning might not be desirable. Later statements make it far more abundantly clear that what is most at stake is methods and motivations, and that these are the factors to be taken particularly into account in making judgments of conscience about family planning. Father Curran, however, as early as 1964 was already envisioning change, by which it is clear that he means simple reversal of what the Church had earlier taught. At that stage (in 1964) those who were postulating the possibility of change were still, for the most part, putting it into terms of development. This was true of Father Curran as well. Those who argued against the acceptance of artificial birth control saw that there was a real problem in that such a reversal would not be development at all. Father Curran, in comparing his earlier to his later position says:

> I in no way mean to impugn the integrity and honesty of those

(myself included!) who used the theory of historical development to explain how the Catholic church could change its teaching on artificial contraception. I feel quite sure that this theory was proposed in good faith by its adherents. However, those who argued against the acceptance of artificial contraception in the Roman Catholic Church in the 1960s recognized the more radical nature of the problem . . . One must honestly recognize that "the conservatives" saw much more clearly than "the liberals" of the day that a change in the teaching on artificial contraception had to recognize that the previous teaching was wrong.

Once *Humanae vitae* was issued and the older teaching reaffirmed, those opposed to it could no longer call upon a theory of historical development. However, there were ways in which the encyclical's condemnation of artificial contraception could be interpreted so that one could mitigate its teaching without at the same time accusing the pope of being in error. From my perspective it was imperative then to take the more radical approach. The teaching condemning artificial contraception is wrong; the pope is in error; Catholics in good conscience can dissent in theory and in practice from such a teaching.[20]

The impression one gets is that Father Curran (and probably many others) had made up their minds long since, and had come to the conclusion that the Church was simply wrong. That may not have been clear in the earlier days, but it is quite clear in the preceding passage. It is difficult to see how this could ever lead to further dialogue. In fact, it seems a clear example of what the theses of the Theological Commission had warned against: "If a person 'unilaterally' claims the whole field of the dialogue, he violates the rules of discussion."

The same theses spoke of coercion and threat as means of destroying real dialogue. I think they may there have been referring to possible misuses of hierarchical authority and were rightly warning against that. At the same time, such things as coercion are not unique to official authority. There is such a thing as the threat of public opinion, which can be brought to bear by the right manipulation of events and opinions. This is, perhaps, indicated in what Father Curran referred to earlier as an unsuccessful attempt to stop the issuing of the encyclical by means of publicity. Anyone who can remember back to that time is certainly aware of just how much adverse publicity there had been. History will, I suspect, conclude to the great credit of Pope Paul VI in not yielding to that sort of pressure. It would have been easy to do nothing; he chose to speak out and reaffirm the teaching of the Church.

The whole account that Father Curran gives of the reaction to the encyclical is, in fact, an account of a public relations effort and not a matter of theology at all. Note the things that are emphasized in his own words: "publicity . . . head-

113

lines . . . television media . . . press conferences . . . as much coverage as possible."
The goal was to see to it that Catholics would get their knowledge of dissent from
the morning papers! This is *not* theology. Authentic ideas of not accepting something in papal teaching are in need of considerable nuance. Father Curran says
that he thought that both laity and priests were largely unfamiliar with such a
notion. To attempt to communicate something so delicate through the media of
newspapers and television is really to do a serious injustice to the Church and its
members—it is a frighteningly irresponsible approach. In fact, theologians had
spoken often enough in the past of situations in which one might find himself in
disagreement with papal teaching and what steps one could take in regard to
this.[21] This is not what Father Curran was doing. Instead, in his own words, he was
involved in "organized dissent." It is an example of a political sort of manuever
designed to bring increased pressure on the "opposition." Again it seems an
instance of what the previously quoted theses warned against: "Wherever the
dialogue becomes an 'instrument' for gaining some end 'politically,' that is, by
applying pressure and ultimately abstracting from the question of truth, the effort
is bound to fail . . ."

When I examine the factors involved in the events described, I am left with
the distinct impression that I am seeing the work of a press agent rather than a
theologian—the creation of a media event and not a search for truth. In my
opinion, this is not the way in which the life of the Body of Christ is to be lived. It
seems to view the whole reality from a perspective that is political and, to some
extent, purely rational. Perhaps not even rational but emotional. It is not the
perspective of faith. Please understand, I am not even attempting to imply anything about anyone else's faith. I am simply stating the point of view from which I
see it.

When Father Curran finds himself ruffled at the accusation that he and the
other theologians did not first read the encyclical before responding to it, I have
some sympathy with him since he did indeed, as he says, read it. But many of
those who signed the response he prepared did not read it first, and he knew
this—he encouraged it! Furthermore, I have some qualms about accepting an
afternoon's heated perusal of a complex document as being serious study. That is
why I do not sympathize with him about the accusation of being precipitate. He
was, both from the viewpoint of not offering people time to examine the encyclical
and from the viewpoint of trying to assure that dissent would arrive with break-
fast. There is, I agree, no real virtue in delay for the sake of delay. There can be
considerable virtue in delay for the sake of time for thought and the welfare of
others.

In recent months Father Curran has again been in some conflict with authority in the Church. Again, there seem to be the techniques of publicity and public
support, rather than the sort of convincing argument that should be the hallmark
of the theologian. I feel sorry about this, because I think that it helps neither
Father Curran nor the Church.

The use of dissent as a tool for creating public opinion or as a means of attempting to make a theological statement has inherent and serious drawbacks, even apart from those already indicated. This is especially the case when one tries, even in part, to found his theological arguments for a position on the basis that there is an already existing dissent within the Church. Cardinal Ratzinger has a pertinent and very interesting comment on this:

> What I find all the more odd about this method of polling people who dissent, is that it is often used by those very theologians who organized the dissent in the first place. If a theologian succeeds in getting his opinion across to even a considerable number of people who happen to be Catholics, it does not yet follow that the argument which preceded the dissent is justified by that subsequent dissent. The widespread dissent is not a *proof* for the dissenting theologian, but it *may* be his *fault*.[22]

I have still one more point to make. This is in reference to the possibility of making judgment about just who is or is not to be viewed as a *Catholic* theologian. Again, I must refer to a statement made by Father Curran:

> According to the commonly accepted application of the principles [of academic freedom] to Catholic institutions, the role of the hierarchical teaching office must be recognized, but ultimate judgments about academic competence or fitness to teach theology must be made by academics and not by any other person or institution. The teaching office, if it deems it necessary, might point out that the work of a particular theologian is problematic or even erroneous, but only that theologian's academic peers can judge his or her ultimate competence to teach Catholic theology in the university in the light of what it means to be a Catholic theologian.[23]

This statement is, to say the least, most seriously misleading. It implies that theology is a law unto itself. The hierarchy has no place in any sort of theological judgment, even a judgment as to who represents the Church and who does not. I don't have any serious argument with the idea that those in the realm of academics may be good, although perhaps not always the best, judges of who is a capable teacher. But judgment as to whether one is a *Catholic* teacher not only can but *must* include the judgment of more than academics. Otherwise the whole question of any relationship between theologians and the Magisterium simply evaporates. I do not know if Father Curran was really fully serious in the just quoted statement (although the tenor of the article leads me to believe he was), but the implications of it seem so obviously in error that I need comment no further. Indeed, I fear that this statement, as well as some others, falls into the category of rhetoric rather than serious discussion.

What must the hierarchical authority of the Church do in a case of real confrontation? We have already seen in the theses the suggestion of a gradual process without precipitate threats or sanctions. In view of the fact that there has been conflict of such proportions since at least 1968, an action by the Church at this point would not seem precipitate. Even in the case of Father Curran, the exchange of letters between himself and the Congregation for the Doctrine of the Faith dates back to 1979.[24] The Magisterium has its own serious responsibility to exercise within the Body of Christ, and part of that responsibility is the burdensome task of making judgments. At the focal point of such judgments is frequently the Church's Congregation for the Doctrine of the Faith, whose present Prefect is Joseph Cardinal Ratzinger. In an address at St. Michael's College in Toronto, 15 April, 1986, he spoke of the relationship between theology and Magisterium. He spoke of the need for the proper freedom for both, emphasizing that the link between them should never come to the point at which it could go to either extreme: That theology be divorced from Magisterium or that it simply idolize Church teaching.

He emphasizes the need to safeguard the freedom of the teacher of theology, but he goes on also to say: "The freedom of the individual instructor is not the only good under the law nor is it the highest good to be safeguarded here."[25] There is the primary task of the preserving and teaching of the faith. This he suggests should be the real rule of thumb for the theologian: That he care for the faith of the simple, the disciples. He says:

> When one teaches, not on his own authority, but in the name of the common subject, the church, the assumption is that he recognizes this fundamental rule and freely obliges himself to observe it. This is so because his opinions are given a weight which they could not possibly deserve on their own, precisely because he teaches on behalf of the church. Believers have confidence in the church's word and so naturally transfer that confidence to those who teach in her name.
>
> One hears a great deal today about the abuse of power within the church. Almost reflexively, there comes to mind the abuse committed by those in authority, and this is certainly possible. But little is said about another abuse of authority, namely the abuse of the authority which the teacher has. This abuse is committed whenever that teacher exploits his students by using a position which the church gave him in the first place to encourage them to accept positions which are opposed to the teachings of the church. In this situation it is also true that church authorities can abuse their power, but not in the way most people think. In this situation, church authorities would abuse their authority if they were to serenely allow this paradoxical situation to continue, and thus lend

their authority to support positions which the church has no authority, no revelation, no promise, no competence to maintain. The care of the faith of the "little ones" must always be more important than the fear of some conflict with the powerful.[26]

The Church's position on the hotly controverted issues of the present (such as abortion, homosexuality, contraception, etc.) has not been ambiguous. Documents in these areas are quite clear. What has seemed to many to be ambiguous is the relationship between the Magisterium which presents its teaching in those documents and some theologians who reject them and yet claim to teach in the name of the Church. This is truly an unfortunate kind of problem because its resolution can so easily hurt people. Yet it is not a problem that can be ignored indefinitely. To allow time to seek solutions peacefully is indeed a necessity, even though that same passage of time seems so often to allow for deeper division as well. Still, it is better to err on the side of charity. Yet there comes a time when charity itself demands the clear and final decision.

The best solution is the one which creates unity, but that solution can only come about with the greatest of good will—something which, with God's grace, is by no means impossible. This sort of solution emerges all the more easily as we recognize the reality of our unity in Christ and live it fully. Yet we are redeemed sinners living in a still imperfect world. Cardinal Ratzinger said:

> In summary, I am convinced that when everyone allows himself or herself to be guided by a conscience rooted in conversion to God, there can be no insoluble difficulties, even though this may not obviate all conflicts. The state of the church, the state of theology and the state of their relationship between each other will be so much better if all parties act and think, starting with God; if each individual can say with Paul, "I, but no longer I."[27]

It is essential that our vision of the Church be the vision of Christ himself. It is only from that vantage point that we can really understand the tensions that arise in life and the final unity that should emerge.

Notes

[1]Cf. Glenn Tucker, *High Tide at Gettysburg,* Morningside House, Dayton, 1980, p. 160.

[2]For a brief history of this question and some very good examples of how the development occurred, read Thomas J. O'Donnell, *Medicine and Christian Morality,* Alba House, N.Y., 1976, pp. 46–58.

[3]Pope Pius XII, 24 November 1957, "Prolongation of Life: Allocution to an International Congress of Anesthesiologists," *The Pope Speaks* 4:393–398. Quoted by Ashley and O'Rourke, *Catholic Health Care Ethics: A Theological Analysis,* St. Louis, 1982, p. 384.

[4]The following are books used in the preparation of this chapter, in addition to those in preceding notes: Various authors, *Moral Theology Today: Certitudes and Doubts,* Pope John Center, St. Louis, 1984; Lucio Brunelli, "Ad alta quota

col Prefetto della Fede," an interview with Cardinal Ratzinger in *Trenta Giorni*, May 1985, pp. 8–17; Charles E. Curran and Richard A. McCormick (eds.), *Readings in Moral Theology No. 3: The Magisterium and Morality*, Paulist Press, 1982; Charles E. Curran, *Ongoing Revision: Studies in Moral Theology*, Fides Publishers, Notre Dame, 1976; *Ibid*, *Transition and Tradition in Moral Theology*, University of Notre Dame Press, Notre Dame, 1979; *Ibid*, "Anxiety in the Academy," *The Tablet*, 9 November 1985, p. 1177; Austin Flannery, O.P., *Vatican Council II: The Conciliar and Post Conciliar Documents*, St. Paul Editions, Boston, 1975; *Ibid*, *Vatican Council II: More Post Conciliar Documents*, St. Paul Editions, Boston, 1982; James Hitchcock, "The American press and birth control: Preparing the ground for dissent," *Homiletic and Pastoral Review*, July 1980, pp. 10–26; James J. Mulligan, *The Pope and the Theologians: The Humanae Vitae Controversy*, Mt. St. Mary's Seminary Press, Maryland, 1968; Francis A. Sullivan, S.J., *Magisterium*, Paulist Press, N.Y., 1983; Joseph Cardinal Ratzinger, "The Church and the Theologians," *Origins: NC Documentary Service*, May 8, 1986, Vol. 15: No. 47, pp. 761–771.

[5]John C. Ford, S.J., and Gerald Kelly, S.J., "Doctrinal Value and Interpretation of Papal Teaching," *Readings in Moral Theology No. 3*, pp. 8–9 (originally in *Contemporary Moral Theology I*, Newman Press, 1958).

[6]*Ibid.*, p. 9.

[7]*Ibid.*

[8]Joseph Cardinal Ratzinger, "Epilogue," in *Moral Theology Today*, pp. 341–342.

[9]This document and commentary can be found in *Readings in Moral Theology No. 3*, pp. 151–170.

[10]Cf. Sullivan, *op.cit.*, pp. 174–176.

[11]Cf. Vatican II, *Gaudium et Spes*, nn. 50, 51,52, 87.

[12]Flannery, *op.cit.*

[13]Curran, *Ongoing Revision*, pp. 260–294.

[14]*Ibid.*, p. 268.

[15]*Ibid.*, p. 279.

[16]*Ibid.*, p. 280.

[17]*Ibid.*

[18]*Ibid.*, p. 281.

[19]*Ibid.*, p. 293.

[20]Curran, *Transition and Tradition in Moral Theology*, pp. 45–46.

[21]Cf. pertinent articles in *Moral Theology Today* and the relevant sections of Sullivan, *Magisterium*.

[22]Ratzinger, *loc.cit.*, p. 3342.

[23]Curran, *Tablet*, p. 1177.

[24]Brunelli, *op.cit.*, p. 10.

[25]Ratzinger, *Origins*, p. 769.

[26]*Ibid.*, pp. 769–770. In conjunction with the passage quoted in the text, it is interesting to note that Father Curran also finds the present situation undesirable. He speaks of a situation in which the *modus vivendi* of many Catholics is not in accord with the teaching of the Church. He says: "I strongly insist that the present situation should not continue. The hierarchical teaching office cannot have it both ways. The present situation in which the official teaching and the accepted practice are so different cannot continue. I am willing to recognize there will always be gaps between promise and performance in the Christian life for all of us. Likewise there will always be tension between teaching the way of the Lord and at the same time showing mercy to those who are not able to fully respond to this teaching. However, the hierarchical teaching authority cannot say one thing in theory and tacitly acknowledge another in practice. Although achieving a kind of peace, the present situation also involves some glaring problems and inconsistencies which call for it to be changed." (Curran, Transition *and Tradition*, p. 53). It is nice to see Father Curran and the Magisterium in agreement in principle, although I suspect that the solution he would like will be different than that to be proposed by the Magisterium.

[27]*Ibid.*, p. 770.

Chapter 9

Resolutions

The earlier chapters of this book were written during the Spring and Summer of 1986. After their completion there began the process of resolution of some of the conflict between Father Curran and the Magisterium. On Monday, August 18, Archbishop James A. Hickey of Washington, as Chancellor of the Catholic University of America, presented to Father Curran a letter received from Joseph Cardinal Ratzinger, Prefect of the Congregation for the Doctrine of the Faith. At the same time the Archbishop notified Father Curran that, in view of the letter from the Congregation, he was initiating the process for removal of the Canonical Mission to teach.

Cardinal Ratzinger's letter pointed out the fact that Father Curran occupied the post of a Professor of Theology in an Ecclesiastical Faculty at a Pontifical University. It was in light of this particular position that action was now being taken. For many people it seems that one of the first obstacles to an understanding of what has happened may relate to the use of unfamiliar terminology; so it might be best, before all else, to clarify our words.

In 1979 Pope John Paul II promulgated an Apostolic Constitution entitled *Sapientia Christiana*. The topic of the constitution was ecclesiastical universities and faculties. The words "ecclesiastical faculty" or "ecclesiastical university" have a very clearly defined meaning, which is explained in the constitution itself. Ecclesiastical universities and faculties are those which are set up by or given special approval of the apostolic See. They teach sacred doctrine and the other bodies of knowledge associated with that doctrine and are given the right to confer ecclesiastical academic degrees. In other words, they are very specially concerned with the teaching of the doctrine of the Church, and they are publicly recognized as occupying an approved and endorsed position within the Church. It is clear that a teaching member of such an institution would have both the privilege of teaching in the name of the Church and a most serious responsibility in the exercise of such an office.

Qualifications for teachers in such institutions include their wealth of knowledge, the testimony of their own way of life and a sense of responsibility. They are expected to have the required degrees and accomplishments that one would expect of scholars, and they must have the ability to teach. The seriousness of this position is further indicated by what is referred to as a "canonical mission." This is a specific appointment or mission to be conferred by the Chancellor of the University. The reason for such a special commission is that it indicates the teacher so designated as one who acts not only on his own authority, but in accord with a special mission granted by the Church. All of what I have been describing in the last few paragraphs can be found in the Constitution itself, and I would suggest that the reader obtain a copy of it and study it carefully.

The one who grants a specific mission to another can also remove that mission as well. This is what has happened in the case of Father Curran. The basis for removing the mission was explained in letters to Father Curran on September 17, 1985, and July 25, 1986 (this being the letter that was delivered in August). In the second appendix to this present book you can read the text of the most recent letter. The earlier letter was made public by Father Curran in March of 1986 and can be read in full or in summary in the various written media.

Father Curran's moral teachings differ, and have differed for some time, from those of the Church's Magisterium. In the last chapter some of these differences were clearly indicated. It is not, however, my intention at this point to enter into discussion on the moral issues involved. For the moment, as in the rest of this book, I am much more concerned with the problem that emerges in terms of the conflict between a theologian and Magisterium itself. Yet there are some most important insights that it would be well to consider. The impression has been given, both in Father Curran's writings and in the press coverage of these past few months, that this is a question of conflict between authority and reason. One would think that Father Curran's moral positions are founded in the scholarly evidence of reason, while those of the Magisterium are an exercise of authority holding on to unreasoned positions of the past. Nothing could be further from the truth. Father Curran gives reasons for what he holds. So too does the Magisterium. Many reputable, scholarly and learned theologians differ from Father Curran in these areas, and do so on the basis of solidly structured reasoning. What the Magisterium contributes to this is not simply authority, but the weight of a long-standing and unambiguous tradition, which happens to be in accord not with what Father Curran presents but with what is and has been presented in the arguments of his opponents in the theological arena. Both sides present reasoned arguments, but those of Father Curran not only are not finally convincing, but neither are they in accord with the already common teaching of the Church.

Enough, however, for such discussion at the present moment. The real issue—the issue which gets beclouded by cries of loss of academic freedom or cries of authority versus reason—is actually quite clear and relatively simple.

Father Curran is and has been in disagreement with a number of the Church's moral teachings—teachings supported by tradition and reason both. At the same time Father Curran is a member of an ecclesiastical faculty of theology is a pontifical university. He occupies a position in which he has been granted a very specific and particular authority as a teacher. This is more than whatever he can claim as the personal authority of the learned academic. It is, in fact, the delegated authority of the Church itself, extended to him in and through the Church.

His divergence from the moral teaching of the Church began many years ago, as we have already seen in the preceding chapter. Those who exercise authority in the Church have proceeded slowly, carefully and considerately in their years of contact with Father Curran. This is as it should be. The Church's concern is not that of simple reaction to error, but real pastoral care for the individual. For at least the past seven years there has been correspondence, discussion, examination and dialogue. In the end it came down to a clear and easy to grasp question. Father Curran had been asked (in September of 1985) whether he does or does not wish to teach what the Church teaches in the controverted areas. If he wished to do so, then the Church would continue to extend to him its approval—its mission to teach in its name. If he does not so wish, then the Church can and should withdraw that specific sort of approval.

Father Curran considered these questions for some months and then communicated to the Congregation his decision that he will continue to hold and teach what he has been holding and teaching. He finds that he cannot agree with the teaching of the Church. The Congregation has responded by saying that it must advise the Chancellor that Father Curran can no longer teach in its name. This is what Cardinal Ratzinger is saying when he says that Father Curran can "no longer be considered suitable nor eligible to exercise the function of a Professor of Catholic Theology." He is not saying that Father Curran is not a Catholic. He is passing no judgment upon the internal state of his conscience. He is merely saying that he cannot officially be considered a Catholic theologian, in the sense of approval which such a title would suggest.

This decision is not in any way an infringement of Father Curran's conscience, nor is it an infringement on his freedom. It is, in fact, the exact opposite. It is a recognition of a conscientious choice on the part of Father Curran. He has freely and conscientiously chosen to disagree with constant and commonly accepted teaching of the Church. The Church, in respect for his conscience, does not say that he must be silent, nor that he must never write on these topics, nor that he must say what he himself does not believe. The Church can and does respect such a decision. But the Church, in the persons of those who must act in its name, must also be true to its conscience and must act in its freedom as well. It must accept his final decision and withdraw the support of its authority in his teaching function. It must say, "We cannot enter into your conscience. We cannot coerce your freedom. But we also cannot act so as to give the impression that what you teach is being taught in our name as well. Let us, for the sake of all concerned, be clear. You teach as you will and as you truly believe, but do not do it as though such teaching comes from authority." In fact, this would seem to be practically the only possible course that the Church could take if it is to respect the rights of the individual, care for the teaching of the faith and act with the degree of responsibility that must be a hallmark of the Church of Christ.

Finally, I would emphasize that the discussion which surrounds both the moral teaching and the conflict between theologian and Magisterium cannot be taken as a condemnation of the person of Father Curran. It is all too easy for all of us, in the heat of argument, to begin by dealing with reasons and end in anger toward a person. If correction is to be the fraternal correction demanded by Christ himself, then it must be done in the light of His love. If we think that someone is wrong, then in charity we must attempt to correct. The purpose is not to win an argument, but to arrive at the truth; not to cause division, but to restore unity; not to justify ourselves and our positions, but to express as fully as possible the teaching of Christ Himself.

Chapter 10

Appendix: No. 25 of *Lumen Gentium*

[The passage as given below is taken from Austin Flannery, O.P. (ed.), *Vatican Council II: The Conciliar and Post Conciliar Documents*, St. Paul Editions, Boston, 1975, 1980, pp. 379–381.]

"25. Among the more important duties of bishops that of preaching the Gospel has pride of place. For the bishops are heralds of the faith, who draw new disciples to Christ; they are authentic teachers, that is, teachers endowed with the authority of Christ, who preach the faith to the people assigned to them, the faith which is destined to inform their thinking and direct their conduct; and under the light of the Holy Spirit they make that faith shine forth, drawing from the storehouse of revelation new things and old (Mt. 13:52); they make it bear fruit and with watchfulness they ward off whatever errors threaten their flock (cf. 2 Tim 4:14). Bishops who teach in communion with the Roman Pontiff are to be revered by all as witnesses of divine and Catholic truth; the faithful, for their part, are obliged to submit to their bishops' decision, made in the name of Christ, in matters of faith and morals, and to adhere to it with a ready and respectful allegiance of mind. This loyal submission of the will and intellect must be given, in a special way, to the authentic teaching authority of the Roman Pontiff, even when he does not speak *ex cathedra* in such wise, indeed, that his supreme teaching authority be acknowledged with respect, and that one sincerely adhere to decisions made by him, conformably with his manifest mind and intention, which is made known principally either by the character of the documents in question, or by the frequency with which a certain doctrine is proposed, or by the manner in which the doctrine is proposed, or by the manner in which the doctrine is formulated.

"Although the bishops, taken individually, do not enjoy the privilege of infallibility, they do, however, proclaim infallibly the doctrine of Christ on the following conditions; namely, when, even though dispersed throughout the world but preserving for all that amongst themselves and with Peter's successor the bond of communion, in their authoritative teaching concerning matters of faith and morals, they are in agreement that a particular teaching is to be held definitively and absolutely. This is still more clearly the case, when, assembled in an ecumenical council, they are for the universal Church, teachers of and judges in matters of faith and morals, whose decisions must be adhered to with the loyal and obedient assent of faith.

"This infallibility, however, with which the divine redeemer wished to endow his Church in defining doctrine pertaining to faith and morals, is coextensive with the deposit of revelation, which must be religiously guarded and loyally and courageously expounded. The Roman Pontiff, head of the college of bishops, enjoys this infallibility in virtue of his office, when, as supreme pastor and teacher of all the faithful—who confirms his brethren in the faith (cf. Lk 22:32)—he proclaims in an absolute decision a doctrine pertaining to faith or morals. For that reason his definitions are rightly said to be irreformable by their very nature and not by reason of the assent of the Church, in as much as they were made with the assistance of the Holy Spirit promised to him in the person of the blessed Peter himself; and as a consequence they are in no way in need of the approval of others, and do not admit of appeal to any other tribunal. For in such a case the Roman Pontiff does not utter a pronouncement as private person, but rather does he expound and defend the teaching of the Catholic faith as the supreme teacher of the universal Church, in whom the Church's charism of infallibility is present in a singular way. The infallibility promised to the Church is also present in the body of bishops when, together with Peter's successor, they exercise the supreme teaching office. Now, the assent of the Church can never be lacking to such definitions on account of the same Holy Spirit's influence, through which Christ's whole flock is maintained in the unity of the faith and makes progress in it.

"Furthermore, when the Roman Pontiff, or the body of bishops together with him, define a doctrine, they make the definition in conformity with revelation itself, to which all are bound to adhere and to which they are obliged to submit; and this revelation is transmitted integrally either in written form or in oral tradition through the legitimate succession of bishops and above all through the watchful concern of the Roman Pontiff himself; and through the light of the Spirit of truth it is scrupulously preserved in the Church and unerringly explained. The Roman Pontiff and the bishops, by reason of their office and the seriousness of the matter, apply themselves with zeal to the work of enquiring by every suitable means into this revelation and of giving apt expression to its contents; they do not, however, admit any new public revelation as pertaining to the divine deposit of faith."

Chapter 11

Appendix: Letter of Cardinal Ratzinger

SACRA CONGREGATIO
PRO DOCTRINA FIDEI
July 25, 1986

Dear Father Curran:

This Congregation wishes to acknowledge receipt of your letter of April 1, 1986 with which you enclosed your definitive reply to its critical Observations on various positions you have taken in your published work. You note that you "remain convinced of the truthfulness of these positions at the present time . . .". You reiterate as well a proposal which you have called a "compromise" according to which you would continue to teach moral theology but not in the field of sexual ethics.

The purpose of this letter is to inform you that the Congregation has confirmed its position that one who dissents from the Magisterium as you do is not suitable nor eligible to teach Catholic Theology. Consequently, it declines your compromise solution because of the organic unity of authentic Catholic Theology, a unity which in its content and method is intimately bound to fidelity to the Church's Magisterium.

The several dissenting positions which this Congregation contested, namely, on a right to public dissent from the Ordinary Magisterium, the indissolubility of consummated sacramental marriage, abortion, euthanasia, masturbation, artificial contraception, premarital intercourse and homosexual acts, were listed carefully enough in the above-mentioned Observations in July of 1983 and since been published. There is no point in entering into any detail concerning the fact that you do indeed dissent on these issues.

There is, however, one concern which must be brought out. Your basic assertion has been that since your positions are convincing to you and diverge only from the "non-infallible" teaching of the Church, they constitute "responsible" dissent and should therefore be allowed by the Church. In this regard, the following considerations seem to be in order.

First of all, one must remember the teaching of the Second Vatican Council which clearly does not confine the infallible Magisterium purely to matters of faith nor to solemn definitions. *Lumen Gentium* 25 states: ". . . when, however, they (the Bishops) even though spread throughout the world, but still maintaining the bond of communion between themselves and with the successor of Peter, and authentically teaching on matters of faith or morals, are in agreement that a particular position ought to be held as definitive, then they are teaching the doctrine of Christ in an infallible manner." Besides, this, the Church does not build its life upon its infallible Magisterium alone but on the teaching of its authentic, ordinary Magisterium as well.

In light of these considerations, it is clear that you have not taken into adequate account, for example, that the Church's position on the indissolubility of sacramental and consummated marriage, which you claim ought to be changed, was in fact defined at the Council of Trent and so belongs to the patrimony of the Faith. You likewise do not give sufficient weight to the teaching of the Second Vatican Council when in full continuity with the Tradition of the Church it condemned abortion, calling it an "unspeakable crime." In any case, the faithful must accept not only the infallible Magisterium. They are to give the religious submission of intellect and will to the teaching which the Supreme Pontiff or the college of bishops enuntiate on faith or morals when they exercise the authentic Magisterium, even if they do not intend to proclaim it with a definitive act. This you have continued to refuse to do.

There are, moreover, two related matters which have become widely misunderstood in the course of the Congregation's inquiry into your work, especially in the past few months, and which should be noted. First, you publicly claimed that you were never told who your "accusers" were. The Congregation based its inquiry exclusively on your published works and on your personal responses to its Observations. In effect, then, your own works have been your "accusers" and they alone.

You further claimed that you were never given the opportunity of counsel. Since the inquiry was conducted on a documentary basis, you had every opportunity to take any type of counsel you wished. Moreover, it is clear that you did so. When you replied to the Congregation's Observations with your letter of August 24, 1984, you stated that you had taken the positions you have "with a great deal . . . of consultation . . ."; and in the Congregation's letter of September 17, 1985, you were actually urged to continue the use of that very means so that an acceptable resolution of the differences between you and the teaching of the Church could be attained. Finally, at your own request, when you came for our meeting on March 8, 1986, you were accompanied by a theologian of your own choosing and confidence.

In conclusion, this Congregation calls attention to the fact that you have taken your dissenting positions as a Professor of Theology in an Ecclesiastical Faculty at a Pontifical University. In its letter of September 17, 1985, to you, it was noted that ". . . the authorities of the Church cannot allow the present situation to continue in which the inherent contradiction is prolonged that one who is to teach in the name of the Church in fact denies her teaching." In light of your repeated refusal to accept what the Church teaches and in light of its mandate to promote and safeguard the Church's teaching on faith and morals throughout the Catholic world, this Congregation, in agreement with the Congregation for Catholic Education, sees no alternative now but to advise the Most Reverend Chancellor that you will no longer be considered suitable nor eligible to exercise the function of a Professor of Catholic Theology.

This decision was presented to His Holiness in an audience granted to the undersigned Prefect on the 10th of July of this year and he approved both its content and the procedure followed.

This Dicastery also wishes to inform you that this decision will be published as soon as it is communicated to you.

May I finally express the sincere hope that this regrettable, but necessary outcome to the Congregation's study might move you to reconsider your dissenting positions and to accept in its fullness the teaching of the Catholic Church.

Sincerely yours in Christ,
/s/ Joseph Cardinal
Ratzinger
Prefect

BIBLIOGRAPHY

The following is a list of the books and articles that were consulted in the preparation of this book.

Anonymous, *The Cloud of Unknowing*, William Johnston (ed.), N.Y., 1973.

Ashley, Benedict M., and O'Rourke, Kevin D., *Health Care Ethics: A Theological Analysis*, St. Louis, Second Edition, 1982.

Bauer, W., *A Greek-English Lexicon of the New Testament* (transs., W.F. Arndt and F.W. Gingrich), Chicago, 1957, 1979.

Beyenka, Sister M. Melchoir, *The Fathers of The Church*, N.Y., 1954.

Bruce, F.F., *New Century Bible: 1 and 2 Corinthians*, Greenwood, S.C., 1971.

Brunelli, "Ad alta quota col Prefetto della Fede," an interview with Cardinal Ratzinger in *Trenta Giorni*, May 1985, pp. 8–17.

Cambier, J., "La premier epitre aux Corinthiens," in *Introduction a la Bible*, (eds.: A. Robert and A. Feuillet), pp. 416–436, Tournai, Belgium, 1957.

Cayre, F., *Manual of Patrology and History of Theology*, 2 Volumes, Paris, 1935.

Cerfaux, L., *The Church in the Theology of Saint Paul*, N.Y., 1963.

Corpus scriptorum ecclesiasticorum Latinorum editum consilio et impensis Academiae Litterarum Caesareae Vindebonensis [CSEL].

Curran, Charles E., *Ongoing Revision: Studies in Moral Theology*, Notre Dame, 1976.

Curran, Charles E. and McCormick, Richard A., (eds.), *Readings in Moral Theology No. 3: The Magisterium and Morality,* N.J., 1982.

Curran, Charles E., "Anxiety in the Academy," in *The Tablet,* 9 November 1985, p. 1177.

Curran, Charles E., *Transition and Tradition in Moral Theology,* Notre Dame, 1979.

Feine-Behm-Kummel, *Introduction to the New Testament,* New York, 1965.

Fitzmeyer, J., "Pauline Theology," in *The Jerome Biblical Commentary* [JBC] (eds.: R.E. Brown, J.A. Fitzmeyer, R.E. Murphy), pp. 800–827, N.J., 1968.

Flannery, Austin, *Vatican Council II: The Conciliar and Post-conciliar Documents,* Boston, 1975.

Flannery, Austin, *Vatican Council II: More Post-conciliar Documents,* Boston, 1982.

Grisez, Germain, *The Way of the Lord Jesus,* Volume I: Christian Moral Principles, Chicago, 1983.

Gunther, J.J., *St. Paul's Opponents and their Backgrounds,* Leiden, Netherlands, 1973.

Hitchcock, J., "The American press and birth control: Preparing the ground for dissent," *Homiletic and Pastoral Review,* July 1980, pp. 10–26.

Jedin, H., *Ecumenical Councils of the Catholic Church,* N.Y., 1960.

Jurgens, W.A., *The Faith of the Early Fathers,* Collegeville, 1970.

Kugelman, R., "The First Letter to the Corinthians," in *JBC,* pp. 254–275.

Latourette, K.S., *A History of Christianity,* N.Y. 1953.

Lewis, C.S., *Mere Christianity,* N.Y., 1943, 1966.

Lewis, C.S., *The Problem of Pain,* N.Y., 1940, 1962.

Lewis, C.S., "Transposition," in *The Weight of Glory,* Grand Rapids, 1966.

MacDonald, George, *Creation in Christ,* (ed.: Roland Hein) Wheaton, Illinois, 1976.

McKenzie J., *Dictionary of the Bible,* Milwaukee, 1965.

Migne, J.P., *Patrologiae cursus completus,* Series prima latina, [ML] Paris, 1844ff.

Mulligan, James J., *The Pope and the Theologians: The Humanae Vitae Controversy,* Emmitsburg, Maryland, 1968.

Musurillo, H.A., *The Fathers of the Primitive Church,* N.Y., 1966.

Newman, J.H., *An Essay on the Development of Christian Doctrine,* Westminster, Maryland, 1845, 1878, 1968.

O'Donnell, Thomas J., *Medicine and Christian Morality,* N.Y., 1976.

Payne, R., *THe Holy Fire,* N.Y., 1980.

Peifer, C., *First Corinthians, Second Corinthians,* Collegeville, 1960.

Quasten, J., *Patrology,* 3 Volumes, Westminster, Maryland, 1960–1962.

Ratzinger, Joseph, "The Church and the Theologians," *Origins: NC Documentary Service,* May 8, 1986, Volume 15: No. 47, pp. 761–1771.

Richardson, A., *An Introduction to the Theology of the New Testament,* N.Y., 1958.

Robinson, J.A.T., *The Body* (No. 5 of *Studies in Biblical Theology*), London, 1963.

Rouet de Journel, M.J., *Enchiridion patristicum loci SS. patrum, doctorum scriptorum ecclesiasticorum quos in usum Scholarum collegit,* [RJ] Rome, 1959.

Sullivan, Francis A., *Magisterium,* N.Y., 1983.

Tolkien, J.R.R., "On Fairy Stories," in *The Tolkien Reader,* N.Y., 1966, pp. 3-73.

Tucker, Glenn, *High Tide at Gettysburg,* Dayton, Ohio, 1980.

Varii, *Conciliorum ecumenicorum decreta,* Rome, 1962.

Varii, *Moral Theology Today: Certitudes and Doubts,* Pope John Center, St. Louis, 1984.

von Campenhausen, H., *Ecclesiastical Authority and Spiritual Power in the Church of the First Three Centuries,* Stanford, 1969.

Wickenhauser, A., *New Testament Introduction,* N.Y., 1963.

Williams, Rowan, *Christian Spirituality,* Atlanta, 1979.

Willis, J.R., *The Teachings of the Church Fathers,* N.Y., 1966.

Wuerl, *Fathers of the Church,* Boston, 1982.

Zerwick, M., *Analysis philologica Novi Testamenti graeci,* Rome, 1953.

Zorell, F., *Lexicon graecum Novi Testamenti,* Paris, 1961.